W9-CDS-885

The Reconstruction of
American Political Ideology
1865-1917

Frank Tariello, Jr.

The Reconstruction *of*
AMERICAN
POLITICAL
IDEOLOGY
1865-1917

University Press of Virginia
Charlottesville

THE UNIVERSITY PRESS OF VIRGINIA
Copyright © 1982 by the Rector and Visitors
of the University of Virginia

First Published 1982

Library of Congress Cataloging in Publication Data
Tariello, Frank.
   The reconstruction of American political
ideology, 1865-1917.

   Bibliography: p. 185
   Includes index.
   1. Political science—United States—History.
I. Title.
JA84.U5T37   320.5'0973   81-14734
ISBN 0-8139-0906-6   AACR2

Printed in the United States of America

CONTENTS

The Reconstruction of
American Political Ideology
1865-1917

INTRODUCTION

The period extending from the end of the Civil War to American entry into World War I was characterized by amazing advances in the natural sciences and technology, hectic industrial expansion made possible in large part by such advances, a considerable improvement in the standard of living, increasing industrial concentration, and growing inequalities in wealth. In a period so dynamic, perhaps the most interesting change of all was that which occurred in American political thought. Whether such a change is to be attributed to the victory of the North in the Civil War and the concomitant triumph of the principles of nationalization and centralization is a moot question.[1] What is certain is that American political theory underwent a remarkable transformation.

The fundamental thesis of this study is that the concept of individualism was radically altered in the post–Civil War era under the impact of the ideology of the progressive movement. Government as a conscious creation of free men, instituted to secure certain preexisting rights and restricted in its sphere of operation, gave way to the notion of an illimitable society as a constantly changing force using government as a tool. The "real" processes of social life and the interplay of interests were substituted for personal autonomy by progressive intellectuals. Inquiry shifted from an examination of government to an anatomy of society. The individual as conceived apart from the collective fell into disrepute.

Such an interpretation, it must be acknowledged, is at variance with many of the secondary analyses of the post–Civil War period. The great majority of these studies are sympathetic to the intellectual revolution wrought by the progressive movement. Consequently, while they trace in general outline the doctrines of reformers, they often only repeat uncritically their arguments. No attempt is usually made, moreover, at a sustained and systematic analysis of the ideas in question. Although the paramount role that the notion of society played in the thought of progressives is frequently admitted, the full implications of the "sovereignty" of society are not drawn. Logical interdependencies among concepts are obscured by concentrating on specific theorists and not on the broad drift of thought.

Common to most interpretations of the post–Civil War period is the belief that the leading reformers of this era rebelled not so much against individualism as against the unwarranted meaning fastened to it. Advocates of the "general welfare state" were seen as altering political doctrine to make it conform to the conditions of a new social and industrial environment. The essence of individualism as understood by the early republicans was preserved; only the form was changed. Henry Commager, for instance, put great emphasis on the clash of theory and practice after the Civil War. He noted that the progressives substituted dynamic for mechanistic concepts, recognized government as a social welfare agency, and pushed for a broad construction of the Constitution. In so doing, they did not desert American tradition, because it was "necessary to clothe ancient rights in modern garments, to supplement traditional freedoms adequate to the pastoral society of the eighteenth century with new ones efficacious in the industrial society of the twentieth." Sidney Fine saw the pre-1865 period as one of laissez-faire and referred to Jefferson and Taylor as advocates of this "negative state" conception. Such a policy was suitable for a "simple agrarian society," yet it was insufficient to meet the demands of an industrial age. Progressives sought, Fine contended, to realize the same objectives of freedom and equality of opportunity valued by the proponents of laissez-faire, only through different means adapted to the conditions of the time. In the final analysis, the general welfare state was a mean between laissez-faire and socialism.[2]

Similarly, Charles Merriam observed that progressives, in meeting the "new conditions of human life," changed liberalism from a political to an industrial form. The general welfare state was simply evolved to deal with problems that the Fathers had not encountered. Ralph Gabriel argued that reformers showed how collectivism could be made the "servant of individualism." Although progressivism was a mixture of different social theories and beliefs, it was a humanistic creed derived from the eighteenth-century Enlightenment. Society was perceived as an "aggregation of individuals," and progressives were rebelling against the gospel of wealth only in so far as it functioned as a defense of "economic government." Merle Curti maintained that radicals and reformers, with the exception of the IWW and anarchists, put their faith in political machinery as the fundamental means of reform and remarked that Edward Bellamy's work helped advance the idea that only under "collectivism could true individualism flourish."[3]

Louis Hartz also posited continuity in American thought. He asserted that the critique of capitalism produced by the antebellum "Southern Reactionary Enlightenment" was quickly forgotten after the Civil War and had only a very small lasting impact on the course of American thought. The presumptions of the proslavery theorists were in no way incorporated into the deliberations of the intellectual critics of the limited state, who adhered to a democratic capitalism. "The post–Civil War theory of democratic capitalism was a pure and absolute antithesis to the philosophy of the Reactionary Enlightenment, and the dreamlike nature of the Southern argument could hardly be better confirmed than by the fact that this philosophy should succeed it and should ultimately influence even the South." Progressivism, Hartz wrote, ruled out by its very nature the concepts of socialism; various social measures were enacted, but they were marginal. The antitrust legislation was pure liberalism and reflected the individualistic bias of the reform movement, which wished to remove the obstacles to individual competition and to "begin running the Lockian race all over again." Furthermore, there were no essential differences between the New Nationalism and the New Freedom, because both were loyal to the democratic capitalist ideology. Although it appeared at times that the reformer was attacking the hallowed values of the national tradition, he was simply reaffirming them. "He advanced a version of the national Alger theme itself, based on trust-busting and boss-busting, which sounded as if he were smashing the national idols but which actually meant that he was bowing before them on a different plane."[4]

Such writers as Vernon Parrington, Daniel Aaron, and Robert McCloskey also have emphasized the compatibility of progressive thought with that of the agrarian republicans, and moreover, they have avowed that the connecting link lies not so much in abstract doctrine as in a real appreciation for human as opposed to property rights. Parrington attested that reformers carried "further the movement inaugurated by the Jeffersonians to make of America a land of democratic equality and opportunity—to make government in America serve men rather than property." Aaron discerned that like their Jeffersonian predecessors, progressives placed "spiritual values above material ones and human considerations above the rights of property." They espoused a philosophy of social experimentation which showed that socialism was not contrary to democracy. Robert McCloskey excoriated the "conservatism" of such men as William Graham Sumner, Stephen Field, and Andrew Carnegie, relating that they unjustifiably welded capitalism to the democratic creed. Acknowledging that "generalizations are perilous," McCloskey pictured Jeffersonian democracy as rooted in spiritual and humane, not material and economic, values. Equality meant equality before God, and liberty was freedom of conscience, not freedom of enterprise. Although republicans never worked out their doctrines systematically, they realized that human rights were superior to the rights of property, the latter possessing only a validity contingent upon circumstances. This conception was perverted by "conservatives" who falsely exalted property as of primary importance. Even Arthur Ekirch, whose viewpoint is hostile to many of the intellectual developments of this era, maintained that at least Wilson's New Freedom, accentuating governmental regulation and antitrust measures, was consonant with individualism, although it bogged down in its own contradictions.[5]

In so far as these interpretations play up, albeit in the broadest terms, some of the characteristics of the democratic collectivism that took form after the Civil War, they are generally correct. To be sure, many specific allegations must be challenged. Contrary to Gabriel, most reformers did not perceive society as simply a collection of individuals. Again, the New Freedom and the New Nationalism were more alike than is sometimes realized; the differences postulated by Ekirch and Aaron were disagreements within a common framework. In addition, it seems incorrect to describe progressivism as a mean between the free market and socialism, thus implying that massive adjustments were not made in theory. In fact, progressivism was unambiguous in its affirmation that society was bound by no inherent limitations in its control over the individual. It also seems questionable to say that Sumner, Field, and other liberals distorted the meaning of individualism so as to justify a predatory materialism, elevating property over human rights. On the contrary, it was their failure to clarify adequately certain crucial issues that made "abstract individualism" seem indefensible, not any alleged desertion of the spirit of Jeffersonianism. Lastly, the notion that agrarian republicans propounded an unadulterated version of laissez-faire, in the meaning usually attributed to that phrase, is inaccurate. These specific objections aside, what is fundamentally defective in these accounts (with the partial exception of that of Ekirch) is the belief that progressives preserved the kernel, or true meaning, of republicanism, while discarding merely its useless husk. It is held as practically self-evident that the transition from an agrarian to an industrial economy necessitated far-reaching changes in political doctrine. These assertions are constantly made, yet they are more often assumed than demonstrated. And it is, perhaps, precisely because they are assumed that a more careful, detailed, and systematic analysis of the relevant problems is not undertaken.

It must be conceded that before we can decide whether the concept of individualism in American political thought suffered a decline, we must embark upon an attempt to define it. We must know what it originally signified, if an informed judgment is to be made as to whether subsequent doctrines conformed to or violated its essence. Now, progressive intellectuals attacked what they believed was established firmly in the American national consciousness, that is, the version of individualism developed by the theorists of revolutionary republicanism.[6] They regarded the early American intellectual tradition as the central "given" that had to be undermined and directed their arguments mainly at what they considered to be its central tenets. This preindustrial individualism, they felt, was the primary obstacle to the erection of an advanced social order. To understand the progressive critique and to be able to evaluate the extent to which the conception of individualism was transformed, we must, first of all, examine republican doctrine.

Much scholarship has been devoted in recent years to the question of the remote origins of the American Revolution and the Constitution, at least partially in the hope that an explanation of their etiology would result in a better understanding of their nature. Such an approach, which has demonsrated the multiplicity, complexity, and crosscutting character of the issues involved, is well founded. Republican individualism, most assuredly, did not spring forth into existence in immediate response to perceived colonial abuses, nor was it the exclusive product of minds on this side of the Atlantic. It was, rather, an intellectual union of diverse strains of thought rooted in both the Western and classical cultures. The American achievement consisted not so much in philosophical originality, although this element was not entirely lacking, as in the elaboration, modification, and application of that venerable body of thought inherited from Europe.

Although the forces shaping republican beliefs and opinions were many, there can be little doubt that the English political experience in all its varigated aspects was the most powerful. The Anglo-Saxon common law tradition, particularly as exemplified in Blackstone and Coke, and the mass of tracts and pamphlets arising specifically out of opposition to the Stuarts and their policies were certainly influential factors. So, too, were the individual contributions of an illustrious line of writers, among whom may be mentioned especially Harrington and Milton. Even more important was that intellectual movement, commonly referred to as the Enlightenment, which, originating in seventeenth-century England and subsequently spreading to the Continent, transformed the soul of the West. The notable efforts of many distinguished authors can be cited here; yet it was indubitably John Locke who played the preeminent role. His impact upon the American republicans and, indeed, upon the whole development of classical liberalism was impressive, and it was exercised directly through his writings and indirectly through the labors of numerous epigoni.

Essentially composed, as we now know, before the advent of the Glorious Revolution, the Lockean analysis assumed as readily self-evident the existence of separate individuals, made a clear and emphatic distinction between society and state, and founded government on the bedrock of consent. Most of all, it furnished an encompassing and thoroughgoing treatment of natural law, one which, in many significant respects, ran counter to the cogtations of Hobbes, and later Rousseau, on the same subject. For Locke, human rights were categorical moral norms applicable to each and every man, prohibiting the use of force by one member of society against another and thereby safeguarding person and property. They were derived from no other source than nature; neither individual whim, as in its Hobbesian guise, nor collective human authority, as in the form of Rousseau's general will, was responsible for their existence. Stripped of its aura of divinity and possessing no more powers than what was conceded to it, the state was merely an agent of its citizens, a mechanical and artificial contrivance designed to remove men from the inconveniences and parlous conditions of the state of nature, collectively protecting natural rights and undertaking the thorny task of translating them into their proper civil equivalents. It most definitely was not an organism compelled to follow, come what may, its own laws of progression, overriding right and the rule of law in the process. As for equality and democracy, Locke, completely in accord with his general orientation, gave to both of them meanings rather restricted in scope, at least in comparison to twentieth-century usage of the terms. Democracy was made to refer to majority rule (however that majority be construed), equality simply to an identity of rights and the supremacy of the law. The belief that the former should denote an omnipotence enjoyed by the people and the latter coercive socioeconomic leveling found no place in his thought.

It was principally from these Lockean motifs, and secondarily from the ideas propounded by a host of pre-Enlightenment writers and the philosophy reflected in common law decisions, that republican votaries in America drew their inspiration. Their selectively eclectic synthesis was informed throughout by a keen appreciation of the irreducible differences between the governmental and the social. Moreover, it was their awareness of the capability of the political element to mold, within limits, human behavior, coupled with the realization that a sincere profession of liberal principles had not spared English society from the ravages of corruption,[7] that induced them to formulate, and provide a justification for, an intricately complex political structure, one whose features have acquired just renown throughout the world. The concept of a written constitution was of the utmost importance here, for it denoted a charter of power defining that structure. Government was to be limited in its sphere of operation not only by its patent obligation to refrain from violating the rights of men but also by its responsibility to remain faithful to the basic principles of the polity as laid down by the constitution. That these principles could not be overturned rightfully even by legislative majorities was seen as a brake on arbitrary exercise of authority and as a safety device against governments which might be tempted to substitute short for long term interests in the name of expediency. In essence, limited government was constitutional government.[8]

The proponents of democratic collectivism[9] by and large rejected republican individualism as sketched here and put forth in its place a notion wholly foreign to it. Basically, society as a constantly evolving organic entity emerged as the starting point of inquiry. Such a tendency was immense in its ramifications. The individual became a derivative product, to be grasped only by studying him in his dynamic relations with others. Government as a deliberate construction designed for specified purposes by individual men became an instrument obediently serving the will of "society as a whole." The public good was construed, not as an interest common to all men within the framework of their natural rights, but as an attribute of a collective entity. Constitutionalism was disparaged in favor of legislative omnipotence, the immediate exercise of majority will; and law was transformed from an objective to an elastic structure, expediency replacing principle. Discussions concerning such matters as the distribution of political power or the meaning of political documents were dismissed as legalistic quibbles of armchair theorists. Reality, reformers asserted, was not to be found in an examination of purely formal relationships. On the contrary, the struggle of social forces and the resulting "equilibrium" constituted the process by which society made known its will. For the progressive, sociology effectively abolished political theory in the meaning usually attached to that term.

The key to all these developments is that barriers which had been erected by the Founding Fathers were dismantled in a freewheeling collectivism which prided itself on being empirical and pragmatic.[10] The essential distinction between government and society broke down, the former becoming a special case of the latter, as critics of the existing order immersed themselves in the study of a vast array of societal phenomena. In fact, it would not be an exaggeration to say that political concepts, those pertaining exclusively to the relationship between man and government, were "socialized." Innate individual rights yielded to social demands sanctioned by the community. Equality before the law was transformed into as great an equality of possessions and social status as might be "practical." Industrial or economic democracy supplanted the republican notion of democracy as political representation of the people. Force was transmuted into "legitimate" aspirations or values denied realization by private acts of commission or omission, even if physical coercion was not involved. Constitutional checks and balances ultimately were replaced by an equilibrium among contending social groups. Essentially, it may be said that the autonomy of politics was destroyed, the public and the private merging indissolubly. In short, free government was displaced by "free society."

Although the progressive ideas quickly acquired popularity, reformers did encounter intellectual opposition in their espousal of the "new individualism." Democratic liberals in the years following the Civil War combated some of the elements of the reformist credo. Yet, they were unable to present a fully logical and convincing defense of limited, constitutional government and proved inadequate to the task of resolving the apparent contradictions and ambiguities in the thought of pre–Civil War republican writers. Many of them disregarded or downplayed critical aspects of the "traditional" concept of individualism, thereby compounding the already existing confusion. And in so far as they, like progressives, tended to ground political prescriptions in sociological theorems, they implicitly abandoned the fundamental distinction between state and society, thereby desiccating their own position. It may be said, then, that they made possible a decline in the concept of individualism, not because they stressed property over human rights or generally deserted the spirit of agrarian republicanism, but because they contributed by default to the victory of democratic collectivism.

This study examines the intellectual synthesis that the critics of free government devised, as well as showing why their opponents were inefficacious. It demonstrates how the pivotal conception of progressive thought, the "socializing" of the political element (based on the prior reification of a dynamic society), manifested itself and with what effects. It is not an exhaustive consideration, or summarization, of the theorizing of the post–Civil War period but selects only those aspects of it germane to the intended purpose. Particularly, it lays bare the inner connections among ideas, treating specific thinkers in the context of the subject matter. From this perspective the breakdown of the allegedly artificial distinction between politics and society can be seen more clearly. To begin with, however, a cursory analysis of the concept of individualism as it appeared in pre-1865 thought, with primary emphasis on republican doctrine, is necessary, so that the rebellion against free government can be placed in greater relief.

CHAPTER I

THE SETTING

Essential to all descriptions of republican individualism as a system of thought is the distinction that republicans drew between society and government. We may go so far as to say that it constituted the fundamental premise of their reasoning, the ideational foundation on which a series of corollary propositions was constructed. Such a distinction may not always have been explicitly made, yet it was always there. Without reference to it, the theorizing of agrarians is not fully comprehensible. Only the acknowledgment of the paramount role it played makes it possible to link together in a coherent fashion the numerous contentions advanced by republican thinkers.

The notion that the private could be separated from the public sphere implied the autonomy of politics, its independence from social pressures. Advocates of revolutionary republicanism posited the political element as primary and did not seek to reduce it to economic or social processes. Their central concern was with the building of a rational political order. It would be wholly erroneous, however, to assert that they were unaware of the existence and activity of social groups. Rather, it was this very awareness which led them to attach so much importance to the structure and offices of government. The fear that special interests would make use of government and violate natural rights in so doing was a real one. The solution to the problem of how exclusive interests were to be prevented from extracting unjust privileges from the community embraced the devising of institutional arrangements that would not only secure liberty and the rule of law but also would ascertain the proper demarcation line between society and state. The framework that was to be established, as well as the process by which it was to be created, was essentially political in nature, as were all the cardinal concepts in the theory. In sum, the vision of agrarian republicans was preeminently a political, and not a social or economic, one.

An integral component of republican individualism, natural rights provided the definition of the objects for which government was to be instituted. In this sense, they fixed the boundary line between polity and society. Moreover, they were predicated of the individual, not of any mystical collective or economic group. They were certainly not understood as social claims upon the labor of others or of the community as a whole. On the contrary, they were normative abstractions establishing the legitimate sphere of action of the individual. As such, they pertained to conditions of human welfare, not necessarily results. Natural rights were also held to be eternal and absolute, true at all times and in all places, and even incapable of being alienated by the will of the individual himself. Because they were perceived as natural, they were not regarded as the gift of society or the state or of any human agency whatsoever. The function of government, therefore, was to secure these rights, not to create them, to ensure their enjoyment, not to abridge them. "Man did not enter into society to become *worse* than he was before, nor to have fewer rights than he had before, but to have those rights better secured. His natural rights are the foundation of all his civil rights."[1]

The hypothesizing of natural rights as anterior to the formation of government and as its base relegated political society to an ancillary status, a simple instrument designed to implement the rights of the individual. And as the means could not contradict the end, the creation of political order could not, in justice, entail the destruction or modification of any of the natural rights possessed by the free individual. The establishment of the state involved the delegation of the individual's right of self-defense to the government and in no way insinuated that the citizens were to become its slaves, deprived of rights and enjoying only such privileges as the rulers thought expedient. "The individual, then, lost neither his freedom nor his independence as a member of society; they were, rather, established for each and all on a surer basis."[2]

The belief that republicans subordinated the right to property to human rights and that their differences with their antagonists inhered in the inferior status which they assigned to material possessions has been argued by some writers.[3] In the light of the evidence, this assertion must be recognized as untenable. Natural rights were frequently enumerated differently by different theorists, yet common to all such enumerations were both the right to personal liberty and the right to property. These two general classes of rights were not regarded as mutually contradictory. Both were strongly affirmed and were not held to be dependent on shifting circumstances. The claim that property was only a contingent right cannot find support in an examination of the writings and statements of leading republicans.

Thomas Jefferson, for instance, took the basis of republican government to be the "equal right of every citizen, in his person and property." Characteristic of his attitude was his remark that a "right to property is founded in our natural wants, in the means with which we were endowed to satisfy these wants, and the right to what we acquire by those means without violating the similar rights of other sensible beings." He explicitly opposed a redistribution of wealth by political power to produce a greater equality of possessions. In this respect, Joseph Dorfman has observed that Jefferson wished to include a note in Destutt de Tracy's *Treatise on Political Economy* (1817), which he had selected to be employed as a textbook at the University of Virginia, to the effect that "the use of the taxing power to correct inequalities of wealth violated the first principle of society, 'the guarantee to every one of a free exercise of his industry and the fruits acquired by it.' "[4] Jefferson fully approved of Tracy's book in which the right to property was dependent upon the personality.[5]

The radical democrat Thomas Paine also did not deny that property was a legitimate right of mankind. He considered it as both a natural and civil right and agreed with Locke that the protection of property was the primary purpose of government. "Every man wishes to pursue his occupation, and enjoy the fruits of his labor, and the produce of his property, in peace and safety, and with the least possible expense. When these things are accomplished, all the objects for which government ought to be established are answered." Certain republican theorists even went so far as to state that property and liberty were so closely allied that a rigid distinction could not be drawn between the two. Hence, James Madison maintained that property did not consist in external possessions alone and that if a man is "said to have a right to his property, he may be equally said to have a property in his rights." In fact, property "embraces everything to which a man may attach a value and have a right; and *which leaves to every one else the like advantage.*" From this perspective, the so-called rights of personality, such as those of unhindered expression, may be depicted as property of a special kind, for each individual "has a property in his opinions and the free communication of them."[6]

This line of reasoning was developed systematically and eloquently by the agrarian John Taylor, sometimes described as the most resolute and impassioned defender of human rights. Man, declared Taylor, has by nature two basic rights, conscience and labor. Although they are analytically separable, a hard-and-fast distinction may not be drawn between them, for there is "no difference between constraints imposed upon the body, and constraints imposed upon the acquisitions of the body." Taylor compared the power of government over thought to that over property, asking rhetorically whether the casuistry is consistent "which denies to a government the power of infringing the freedom of religion, and yet invests it with a despotism over the freedom of property." In essence, he noted that no rights can be exercised if the right to property is violated. To assail it is to assail human life itself. "I cannot see any difference between taking away from a man one of his eyes, if it could be done, and giving it to another; or taking away and giving to another fifty per centum of his labour." The American revolutionaries saw life and liberty as inextricably linked to property, so that the "rights of the latter could not be invaded, without invading the other rights also." Because liberty and property are so intimately connected, had the power to transfer wealth from one man to another been proposed at the time of constitution-making, it would have been rejected with indignation. Indeed, one of the reasons why the Constitution was created to supplant the Articles of Confederation was the transparent injustice of the state legislatures' partial confiscation of private property through the impairment of contracts after the end of the war.[7]

It has been shown that the republicans affirmed the rights of property as well as those of persons and that they did not exalt the latter at the expense of the former. They thought, in Madison's words, that in a "just and free Government . . . the rights both of property and of persons ought to be effectually guarded."[8] Undoubtedly, this creed of natural rights operated as a basic limitation on government, restricting its sphere to their collective protection. The state was not aggrandized at the expense of the individual. Still, the task of giving a concrete meaning to the abstract rights of man in specific situations devolved upon the government. The main problem inhered in the determination of how they were to be implemented in practice. With regard to personal rights, the freedoms embodied in the first ten amendments to the Constitution were commonly held as a general, if not exclusive, enumeration. Translating the principle that man enjoyed a right to property into civil law presented a more vexing difficulty. Spokesmen of republicanism did not imagine this right as implying that some men had to provide others with property or that material possessions, however obtained, could be justified by asserting the right to property.[9] On the contrary, the meaning they fixed to it was that men had the right to acquire and use wealth so long as they did not employ force or fraud in their pursuit of it. In addition, republicans did not avow that physical force could be initiated only by private individuals. They were acutely conscious as well that the state could violate property rights through the imposition of either controls upon the market or excessive and unjust taxation. They did not characterize free and private association as exploitative. It was, rather, the allocation of wealth by law, through whatever mechanism, that was seen as fundamentally destructive of the sanctity of private property. Consequently, agrarians supported freedom of enterprise, the right of individuals to conduct economic transactions on a voluntary basis, according to their own will and judgment, and they spurned a general direction of industry by the state. As H. B. Parkes has attested, the republican conception of the ideal polity precluded the government from forcibly redistributing property, whether in the guise of taxation or by means of political restrictions upon trade.[10]

In this light, it can be seen that the agrarian criticism of Federalist policies was motivated not by the desire to despoil the rich for the benefit of the poor nor by the wish to place human rights above and over those of property. Republicans expostulated repeatedly and vehemently against those governmental incursions into the economy which tended to shift wealth from one geographical section or economic group to another. "Privileged" individuals were those who were the beneficiaries of governmental measures transferring property, not those who simply happened to be more prosperous than their fellow men. Indeed, pervasive, acrimonious conflict was perceived as generated by political and not social factors.[11]

Of all republicans, perhaps John Taylor made the most thorough and extended attack on the policy of bestowing or taking property away by law, designating such a transfer as aristocracy. Adopting a strong states' rights position, he vigorously criticized the assumption of undelegated powers by the central government and legislation that aimed to wed the rich to that government by offering them privileges obtained by application of the public force. The protective tariff, the machinations of the National Bank, and corruption, he felt, were all sapping the strength of the Republic by enriching a class of manufacturers and bankers at the expense of the great majority. It was the federal government which was subsidizing industrialization by a variety of indirect, yet coercive, schemes. Taylor did not call for the plundering of the rich by the poor to right this evil, contending only that no social group should be endowed by law with the power of distributing the fruits of the labor of others, whether such a group was a minority or a majority. "Laws cannot constitutionally transfer the property of debtors to creditors, nor of creditors to debtors, any more than they can transfer that of the rich to the poor or of the poor to the rich. It is our policy, that property should be divided by industry and not by any species of sovereign power; and our judicial departments were established for the preservation of that policy against whomsoever should molest or impair it; and particularly against executive and legislative power, by which the principle has been generally overturned." Although Taylor frequently declaimed against capitalists, he made it clear that what he was objecting to was not the process of free production and exchange but the imposition of political controls upon them supported by many capitalists. He drew no spurious distinctions between labor and capital, maintaining that the worker himself can be regarded as a manufacturer who has as much a right to the products of his labor as the employer does to his. "I freely admit, that capitalists, whether agricultural, commercial, or manufactural, constitute useful and productive classes in society; and by no means design, in the use of the term, to insinuate that it contains an odious allusion. It may even be applied to the man, whose bodily labour is his sole capital. But I also contend, that capital is only useful and reproductive, when it is obtained by fair and honest industry; and that whenever it is created by legal coercions, the productiveness of the common stock of capital is diminished." Capital is, in fact, not to be divorced from labor, for the latter is the only manufacturer and is, therefore, performed by the rich and the poor, the employer and the worker, who obtain their wealth without resorting to coercion or fraud.[12]

Thomas Jefferson and James Madison also inveighed against governmental restrictions on private enterprise and the redistribution of property through legislative fiat. Jefferson insisted that commerce should be relieved of "all its shackles," for "agriculture, manufactures, commerce, and navigation, the four pillars of our prosperity, are the most thriving when left most free to individual enterprise." In a letter to Madison, he went so far as to declare his desire that a prohibition on state-enforced monopolies be included in the Bill of Rights. And his aversion to the National Bank was, in part, motivated by his belief that it infringed the natural laws against monopoly. Madison similarly criticized those who would substitute public for private initiative and averred that industry and labor were most productive when unrestrained. In his opinion, a government which embarked upon a policy of laying restrictions upon trade was not only unwise but unjust as well, for it was thereby abridging the rights of property. "That is not a just government, nor is property secure under it, where arbitrary restrictions, exemptions, and monopolies deny to part of its citizens that free use of their faculties, and free choice of their occupations, which not only constitute their property in the general sense of the word; but are the means of acquiring property strictly so called." In sum, Madison advocated that as a "*general* rule, individuals ought to be deemed the best judges of the best application of their industry and resources."[13]

In like fashion, Thomas Paine identified the right to property with the "liberty of every man to make such a disposition of his possessions, capital, income, and industry as he chooses." He did not lambast free exchange as such. On the contrary, he assailed what he considered to be political fetters upon the marketplace, pointing out that many corporations, by virtue of the privileges granted to them by government, deprived others of their right to acquire property. With regard to the wages of workmen, he asked why they should not be left "as free to make their own bargains, as the law-makers are to let their farms and houses." Like John Taylor, Paine was keen to discern in many governmental policies an indirect transfer of property. In his *Dissertation on Government* (1786), he found fault with the Pennsylvania state legislature's repeal of the charter of the Bank of North America and its attempt to inflate the currency through the issuance of paper money. Paine argued that such a measure would shift wealth from one part of the society to the other by legislative coercion, writing that most of the "advocates for tender laws are those who have debts to discharge, and who take refuge in such a law, to violate their contracts and cheat their creditors." On the whole, his criticism was directed at the debilitating actions of government, not social relationships based on private agreement. It was to the former that he traced most of society's ills. Thus, Paine attributed poverty in Europe to excessive taxation, avouching that "when the taxes were very low, the poor were able to maintain themselves; and there were no poor-rates." Even his proposal to establish old-age pensions was founded not on the right of the government to redistribute wealth but rather on the principle that the taxes which the citizens paid were thereby being remitted in part.[14]

Although republicans regarded the right to property as sacred and understood it as implying both a great measure of freedom in exchange and production and a prohibition against forcible redistribution of wealth, it would be fallacious to say that their views were dogmatically opposed to state intervention of any kind and that they adhered to a laissez-faire creed without any significant modifications.[15] To begin with, they conceded that the government had the right to tax property in order to support its legitimate activities. It was recognized that this power could be abused, yet it was held as indispensable. Moreover, practically all republicans granted that it was the responsibility of government to perform certain crucial service functions that would not be carried out adequately, if at all, by private initiative, primarily education[16] and internal improvements,[17] the necessity of the former being predicated upon the supposition that the experiment in republicanism could have a reasonable chance for success only if the masses were truly enlightened.[18] Others supported certain restraints on the free-dom of trade, most prominently the protective tariff, agreeing with Madison that laissez-faire was a broad guide to policy, not a rigid standard to be applied inflexibly in all cases.[19] Finally, many, if not all, republicans believed that the implementation of property rights necessitated a departure from laissez-faire in certain instances. In particular, they felt that some of the patterns of land ownership inherited from the past either reflected the inequities of the feudal system or were the product of the unjustifiable canon that the first appropriators could exclude all others. Thus, Jefferson protested that when-ever "there is in any country, uncultivated lands and unem-ployed poor, it is clear that the laws of property have been so far extended as to violate natural right," and he insisted that those who could not support themselves be given the "right to labor the earth." From a similar perspective, Thomas Paine, in his *Agrarian Justice* (1797), proposed remedial action by the state to obtain equity for those excluded from access to the soil, advancing his scheme of indemnification funded by a tax on land.[20] One need not agree with these and like suggestions, as many republicans did not, to realize that the objective was to ascertain the boundary line between wealth acquired by honest effort and wealth obtained solely by the appropriation of natural factors,[21] not to create a class indebted to the govern-ment for its existence.

Although departures from the policy of strict noninterven-tion were designed to serve a variety of purposes, the general intention behind them was to construct an institutional frame-work, a favorable environment, in which the individual could advance his interests most effectively and without prejudice to others. None of the particular measures recommended were aimed at abridging property rights by transferring wealth from one class to another. The benefits to be derived, it was hoped, would redound to the welfare of nearly all citizens. Moreover, republicans felt that the exceptions to the rule of freedom of trade were not to be exaggerated or multiplied so indiscrimi-nately that the system of free commerce, in theory or practice, would be overturned and a sweeping regulation of business by the political power substituted for it. Madison, for example, explicitly cautioned against such a development, critically and presciently observing that many of the votaries of the tariff would "convert the exceptions into the rule, and would make the Government a general supervisor of individual concerns."[22]

The concepts of equality, democracy, and the public interest were also crucial components of republican individualism. Again, they were comprehended in a political sense. Equality was used to mean both that the law was to apply uniformly to all men, whether rich or poor, and that men possessed identical rights.[23] The idea of a natural aristocracy of birth entitled to legal privileges was forthrightly repudiated, most notably by John Taylor in his running attack on John Adams. Equality, then, was not a synonym for the division of wealth into equal, or more equal, portions. Nor did it signify that social groups had identical, intrinsic claims to the "national wealth." As for democracy, it pertained exclusively to the participation of the people in selecting the government that would rule them. Republicans commended a democratic form as less likely to produce injustice than one in which an elite monopolized power.[24] By and large, they looked askance at those qualifications for the suffrage, such as property, which would tend to minimize radically the number of electors and sought to prevent the arising of a ruling class with interests different from those of the ruled by bringing government as close to the people as possible. Democracy was not construed as applying to the sphere of private relations, as meaning that social and economic arrangements of a voluntary nature had to correspond to the wishes of a majority of the community even if individual rights were transgressed. Majority rule was not an end in itself, exempt from moral canons, nor could the few be legitimately sacrificed to the many. As Madison put it, "There is no maxim, in my opinion, which is more liable to be misapplied, and which, therefore, more needs elucidation, than the current one, that the interest of the majority is the political standard of right and wrong. . . . In fact, it is only re-establishing, under another name and a more specious form, force as the measure of right."[25] Far from wishing to subject the individual to the absolute rule of a collective, republican theorists were profoundly preoccupied with the problem of reconciling majority rule and the individual's right to be bound by no will but his own.[26]

Some nebulousness, however, did envelop the concept of the public interest, which was never rigorously defined, although often used. Indeed, the very term "public interest" seems to conjure up the image of a superior entity having interests which may or may not coincide with those of individuals. And republicans frequently invoked the general against the exclusive interest. They did not, nevertheless, reify the public or aspire to swallow up the individual in a cryptic collective whose every dictate would have to be obeyed unquestionably. The existence of the individual was accepted as self-evident, and his good was not opposed to that of a fictitious being called the public. "Public good is not a term opposed to the good of individuals; on the contrary, it is the good of every individual collected. It is the good of all, because it is the good of everyone: for as the public body is every individual collected, so the public good is the collected good of those individuals."[27] Natural rights were not subordinated to the public interest, therefore. In fact, there was no inevitable friction between the two. "What is true of every member of the society individually, is true of them all collectively, since the rights of the whole can be no more than the sum of the rights of individuals."[28]

One important implication of this train of reasoning was that the effort of an individual to better his station in life was not a threat to the pecuniary well-being of the whole. There was not a fixed amount of riches possessed by the "community" which had to be apportioned out on a roughly equal basis if exploitation was to be eliminated. Wealth was created by individuals. It would, then, be unsound to maintain that its unequal possession, in so far as it was obtained neither by force nor by fraud, was evidence that some had taken more than their "fair share." The only true basis for a general prosperity was the individual's attempt to produce more wealth. As John Taylor advised, an "endeavor in each to further his own nest, is the only way to procure comfort for all."[29]

Still less was the public interest pictured as an ideological figleaf concealing the warfare of socioeconomic groups struggling for control of the instrument of government. Nor did it denote a policy which benefited a particular interest, even if composed of a majority of citizens, to the detriment of another. John Taylor had spoken very approvingly of the role of the landed interest as a bulwark of the Republic and had upbraided measures that were directed toward producing its political demise and economic impotence. But he did not claim that it was the task of the state to benefit it through subsidization or by injuring the mercantile groups, because the "utmost favour which it is possible for a government to do for us farmers and mechanics, is neither to help nor hurt us."[30] His appreciation of the landed interest was partially grounded on the realization that it was not as susceptible to corruption and easy manipulation as were others.[31] Of course, it is not to be inferred that republicans abjured any state intervention whatsoever pertaining to the interests. Most shared Madison's sentiment that the government's policy should be one of "abstaining from measures which operate differently on different interests, and particularly such as favor one interest, at the expense of another."[32] Legislation that was not prejudicial to any section and was consonant with individual rights was not disdained. What was scorned was the notion that the public interest conferred illimitable power upon the lawmaking body to remake society according to its desires.

The political vision that was at the core of Jeffersonian individualism and that was manifested in its fundamental concepts culminated in what may best be termed "constitutionalism." Limited government basically referred to the fact that the authority of the rulers was circumscribed by a written document which not only embodied in concrete form the rights of the individual but also detailed the rules and procedures by which the polity was to function. To be sure, the people were the fountainhead of power, but this did not mean that the legislature was omnipotent. On the contrary, because the people, and not government, were the creators of the Constitution, legislative sovereignty was nonsensical. "In the first place, in the American *written constitution,* higher law at last attained a form which made possible the attribution to it of an entirely new sort of validity, the validity of a *statute emanating from the sovereign people.* Once the binding force of higher law was transferred to this new basis, the notion of the sovereignty of this ordinary legislative organ disappeared automatically, since that cannot be a *sovereign* law-making body which is subordinate to another law-making body."[33] All enactments of the government that did not conform to the Constitution were regarded as invalid, for "constitutional law . . . is as binding upon political departments, as civil law is upon individuals.[34] Indeed, by definition, legislative power is only the delegated power of making laws "*consistent with the foundation and principles of the constitution.*"[35]

Constitutionalism was a direct reflection of the Jeffersonian belief that government and society composed two separate, autonomous spheres. The notion that the authority of the state should extend to all objects of human concern was rejected. The reductionist view that politics consisted in the struggle of social groups and that it was proper, therefore, for "society" to employ the organs of the body politic to realize its will was not adopted. The realm of politics encompassed what was truly of common interest to the people; beyond this, the state could not go. There remained a sphere in which the individual could fashion his life as he saw fit, in which voluntary social rela-tion-ships were not subject to the use of coercion. The very concept of a constitutional republic, as Isabel Patterson has testified, was an expression of this view. "A Republic signifies an organization dealing with affairs which concern the public, thus implying that there are also private affairs, a sphere of social and personal life, with which government is not and should not be concerned; it sets a limit to the political power."[36]

The principle followed in ascertaining the scope of the state was that the government had only those powers which were explicitly given to it and were embodied in the Constitution. In other words, what was not permitted, was forbidden. It was in this context that republicans vigorously reproved those who would interpret the "general welfare" clause as conferring additional, or even unlimited, functions upon the government. John Taylor, for instance, insisted that the clause in question could not justify the assumption by Congress of undelegated powers. "It follows, either that these words convey no power, or that the subsequent definition of the powers delegated restrict their meaning. In fact, they are obviously introductory, and not decretal." He warned that "no powers can be more sovereign and arbitrary, than those of deciding and doing whatever may administer to the public good." Jefferson concluded that if the common interest could sanction the existence of a national bank as Hamilton had maintained, then the Constitution could be reduced to the statement that Congress could do whatever it thought would be good for the United States. Madison agreed with Taylor that the clause providing for the general welfare was merely introductory and that its meaning had to be sought in the grants of power specifically listed in the text. To construe it otherwise would signify that the government had become unlimited, for if "Congress can do whatever in their *discretion* can be *done by money,* and will promote the *general welfare,* the government is no longer one possessing enumerated powers, but an indefinite one subject to particular exceptions." Particularly, in his veto of a bill providing for the construction of roads and canals by the federal government, Madison repudiated the belief that the common good could sanction the enlargement of congressional powers beyond those cited in the Constitution.[37]

Republicans also castigated Hamilton's doctrine of implied powers as effectively abolishing the Constitution. John Taylor complained that "this new notion of a constitution by implication is, I confess, exactly like no constitution at all." Madison observed that carried to its logical conclusion, it would result in such an extension of the government's authority that the private sphere could virtually be eliminated. "If implications thus remote and thus multiplied may be linked together, a chain may be formed that will reach every object of legislation, every object within the whole compass of political economy."[38] In addition, the companion argument that bald precedent could enlarge the functions of the state was denied. "Government by precedent, without any regard to the principle of the precedent, is one of the vilest systems that can be set up. In numerous instances, the precedent ought to operate as a warning, and not as an example, and requires to be shunned instead of imitated; but instead of this, precedents are taken in the lump, and put at once for constitution and for law."[39]

In this context, it was the desire to restrict government within its proper domain, and not a propensity for mere "legal quibbling," that motivated such republicans as Taylor and Madison to engage in subtle and extended exegesis of the American Constitution. Strict construction was not the idle diversion of ivory-tower philosophers separated from reality; it was the instrument by which limited government was to be preserved. An elastic interpretation, one consulting prevailing social trends or an undefined public good or precedent or majority opinion, was explicitly cast aside as subversive of the survival of the constitutional structure itself.

In summary, the system established by the Founding Fathers, whether one calls it "constitutionalism" or "free government" or "limited government," was preeminently political in conception. It set up a barrier against the use of political power for arbitrary ends by creating a government of enumerated functions. The Constitution was a curb on the state, not on private individuals. It was not a social document in the sense that it was intended to serve as a regulator of the conflicts among various socioeconomic interests. Republican individualism, in all essential respects, was a political creed.

Before proceeding, cognizance should be taken of the caveat raised by some scholars that Jeffersonian individualism did not appertain to state and local government. Those who have adopted such a position frequently stress the extent to which individual states before the Civil War departed from laissez-faire. While such departures have often been exaggerated,[40] the following points should be made. First, agrarians did not write extensively on the appropriate powers that were to be assumed by the states, and it is therefore difficult to ascertain precisely what views they may have held in this regard. Second, it is no more correct to infer the opinions of leading republican theorists on these matters by mechanically scanning the records of state legislation than it would be to deduce their opinions on the proper role of the federal government from the laws approved by the national legislature. Third, there is no evidence to suppose that when republicans characterized government in the abstract as founded in consent, bound by fundamental law, and instituted for the protection of personal and property rights, they intended to confine such characteristics to the central government. Fourth, they believed that those activities constituting exceptions to the rule of laissez-faire, such as internal improvements, were generally best managed and financed by the states. Local benefits were to be derived by taxing local beneficiaries; there was no desire to afford pretexts to the federal government for redistributing wealth among states. Lastly, agrarians realized that the very existence of a multitude of states provided an effective and powerful check upon possible infringements of individual freedom, since American citizens always had the option of leaving a less for a more congenial state. All in all, while they conceded that the states, subject to the restraints imposed on them by the Constitution, were responsible for devising their own constitutions and for defining the content and mode of implementation of human rights, they had no intention of conferring upon them any arbitrary powers. Even as fanatical a states' rights philosopher as John Taylor could fervidly gainsay that any government, or subdivision thereof, had a "sovereignty" over property.[41]

The doctrines of the partisans of free government, although by no means a monolithic whole,[42] did exert a striking influence on American theory and practice before the Civil War. Nevertheless, they encountered intellectual opposition from Federalists, Southern nationalists, and, to a certain degree, Transcendentalists before 1865. While only the doctrines of the last are usually characterized as "individualistic," it would not be amiss to consider very briefly the points at which they departed from revolutionary republicanism.

The extent of the disagreement between Federalists and republicans has often been overstated, particularly by those eager to see in the former the representatives of "privilege" and in the latter the defenders of the common man. There were, of course, Federalists who, following Hamilton, desired an expansion of governmental powers beyond those specified in the Constitution by giving the "general welfare" a broad meaning. They sought to associate the rich with the government in a variety of ways, and their projects frequently entailed the indirect transfer of wealth from one group to another. Many Federalists, however, held basically the same assumptions concerning the ends the political order should promote as the agrarians.[43] Like them, they affirmed that society was no more than the sum of its members, that the individual, the starting point of investigation, possessed natural rights independent of society and state, that the purpose of government was to protect these rights and provide a favorable environment for their exercise, that equality was a political and not a social concept, that force was to be distinguished from private and free association, and that the Constitution should mark off the limits of the powers of the state. Disagreement arose over the political machinery that was to secure the accepted ends. If, as Paine stated, the first criterion distinguishing free government from the despotic is the lodging of sovereignty in the people and the second is its principles, then such Federalists discarded the former in order to maintain the latter. In other words, they separated democracy from liberalism. They may, in fact, be called conservative liberals. They were liberal in that they supported inherent limitations on the scope of government based on natural rights, and they were conservative in that they thought the ideal polity could only be maintained by a quasi-aristocratic ordering. Those who disparaged democracy did so because they believed that it would lead to the triumph of the mob and the institution of majoritarian tyranny. These apprehensions were particularly and candidly reflected in the writings of an eminent conservative liberal, John Adams, who anticipated that in a purely democratic government demagogues would arise to incite the poor against the rich, the final assault on property resulting in an equal division of possessions. Adams's much maligned scheme, the balancing of orders, was intended to prevent majority as well as minority despotism.[44]

Other Federalists, while not accepting Adams's solution, were just as pessimistic about democracy. Acutely cognizant of its shortcomings, they strove to hedge it in with a variety of devices, notably extensive property qualifications for the suffrage. They reasoned that those with property would not attack it and those without it would not have the opportunity to do so, at least by democratic means. Furthermore, they wished to contain the effects of popular rule, either by removing many of the principal offices of the government from any kind of election, making them dependent upon appointment, or by making them subject to indirect election. For similar reasons, they supported a strong executive.[45]

As the years went by and the American democracy showed little sign of degenerating into mobocracy, many Federalists abandoned their antipathy to democracy and became reconciled to the participation of the masses in government. Their position, then, became even closer to that of republicans, and perhaps, as Louis Hartz has suggested, this is why the Federalist party finally met its demise. Southern proslavery theorists and Transcendentalists, however, did challenge various aspects of republican individualism. The former were much more radical and thoroughgoing in their critique, and they had some success, particularly in the South, in discrediting the central tenets of revolutionary republicanism. Interestingly enough, their conclusions were often remarkably akin to those of post–Civil War reformers, although they started from different premises and very little in the way of direct influence can be traced.

Usually portrayed as strongly anti-individualistic in orien-ta-tion, Southern nationalists attempted to defend slavery as a positive good. In so doing, they arrived at an organic concep-tion of society which disparaged the notion of natural rights. George Fitzhugh, for instance, condemning freedom as equiva-lent to anarchy, claimed that the individual "has no rights, whatever, as opposed to the interests of society; and society may very properly make any use of him that will redound to the public good." John C. Calhoun, although he remained a constitutionalist, likewise pushed aside personal rights and stressed the importance of society. He ridiculed the idea of the state of nature, observing that man's "natural state is the social and political."[46] Like Fitzhugh, he set up society as the focus of political inquiry. The significance of all of this was that it constituted a major attack on the very foundations of, and rationale for, free government. If the individual did not enjoy innate rights and could not even be said to exist apart from society, then there would be, in principle, no intrinsic limits on the rulers' sphere of action. Trying to save the institution of black slavery, Southern theorists were, paradoxically, driven to evolve a philosophy which engulfed all, black and white, in bondage to a supraindividual society.

Transcendentalists, on the other hand, adhered to a form of individualism which differed in several respects from the republican conception. They did not, to be sure, deny the existence of natural rights.[47] Nor did they call for a general regulation of economic enterprise in the name of higher truths. Henry Thoreau, in fact, maintained that trade and "commerce, if they were not made of India rubber, would never manage to bounce over the obstacles which legislators are continually putting in their way" and insisted that the American people would have done more if government had not gotten in their path. Furthermore, Transcendentalists did not dissolve the individual in a mystic state or society, for, as Emerson wrote, the "advantage of the whole is best consulted in consulting the real advantage of the particular."[48] Fundamentally, their indi-vidualism differentiated itself from that of republicans by its relatively apolitical orientation. Borrowing from Coleridge, Kant, Schelling, and other European intellectual figures, Transcendentalists developed a philosophy of "intuitionism" which, as they employed it, not only did not lend itself to an immediate and obvious application to political problems but often seemed to justify a retreat from the very stuff of politics itself. They did not attempt to reduce the political to the social, of course. Rather, they simply embraced a philosophical vision which downplayed the state. Hence their failure to develop a comprehensive theory of the polity. Their writings do not contain any searching consideration of many of those issues with which republicans had occupied themselves.

This retreat from politics manifested itself in other ways as well. First, whereas republicans had conceived that government was an abiding necessity and performed useful functions, Transcendentalists frequently branded the state as corrupt and looked wistfully to the day when it would no longer be required. Emerson, for instance, prophesied that the advent of the "wise man" would mean the doom of the state, feeling that "the less government we have the better, the fewer laws, and the less confided power. The antidote to this abuse of formal Government is the influence of private character, the growth of the Individual; the appearance of the principal to supersede the proxy; the appearance of the wise man; of whom the existing government is, it must be owned, but a shabby imitation." Thoreau, while not calling for the immediate abolition of the state, decided that the same arguments which had been brought against the standing army could be brought against government. Second, Transcendentalists averred that the individual had the right to ignore the state. Emerson protested that he could not bring to "mind a single human being who has steadily denied the authority of the laws, on the simple ground of his own moral nature" and urged good men not to "obey the laws too well." Again, Thoreau, though not advocating violence to remedy unjust laws, held that men could rightfully place themselves outside the jurisdiction of government. "I simply wish to refuse allegiance to the State, to withdraw and stand aloof from it effectually." In fact, he declared that government could have no "pure right" over a man's property and person but what was conceded by him to it.[49]

All in all, whereas republican individualism was marked by its intensely political character and stressed the participation of a politically aware citizenry in the affairs of government, the doctrines of Transcendentalists such as Emerson and Thoreau offered a conception of individuality which focused upon the development of human character as a final alternative to the state. Envisioning the ultimate demise of the state and clinging to the right of the individual to "stand aloof" from its dictates, Transcendental individualism was consciously apolitical, and at times even antipolitical, in its orientation.

Most post–Civil War reformers did not borrow directly from Southern proslavery thought, and they were not basically influenced by the standpoint of Transcendentalism. Nor did they aspire to an antidemocratic Federalism. Discovering that republican individualism was propping up the existing state of affairs, they held that before meaningful and necessary changes in the polity could be brought about, the doctrines espoused by republicans had to be intellectually discredited. The ideology which they evolved was designed to serve that purpose, and in many ways the attempt was successful. Can this success be explained, at least in part, by certain inherent flaws in the philosophy of free government? In other words, was agrarianism marred by any weaknesses that helped make its later supersession possible?

While the achievements of republican thinkers must be duly acknowledged, two fundamental defects can be noted. First, they provided no philosophical rationale for limited government. They posited natural rights without any serious effort to derive them from more general propositions. Quite simply, they believed that individual happiness was a goal sought by everyone and that liberty was the means best adapted to this end. But they offered no comprehensive ethical formulas. Jefferson's conjecture of an inborn moral feeling was, perhaps, an endeavor to supply the requisite theorems. He was provably aware of the serious difficulties which such a view entailed and never expatiated upon it. Similarly, the morality of enlightened self-interest was never put on a philosophical basis nor even clearly defined. The American political system, therefore, functioned in an ethical vacuum. Second, there was some ambiguity surrounding the concept of creating that institutional framework in which individuals could develop their talents. Republicans had recommended that government, whether at the state or national levels, support certain service activities, such as education and internal improvements. However necessary such projects might be, it could be objected that, regardless of intention, they resulted in an effective transfer of wealth from one group of individuals to another. Perhaps anticipating this criticism, Madison had explained, pertaining to education, that there could be "little ground for objections from any class to plans of which every class must have its turn of benefits. The rich man, when contributing to a permanent plan for the education of the poor, ought to reflect that he is providing for that of his own descendants; and the poor man, who concurs in a provision for those who are not poor, that at no distant day it may be enjoyed by descendants from himself."[50] It is apparent, nevertheless, that not all would benefit equally or in proportion to their monetary contribution. It would be unjustifiable to say that it would be impossible in principle to reconcile the right to property with the existence of such schemes. Still, a more extended development of the theory at this point would have eliminated a substantial lacuna. Kindred observations apply to the imposition of restraints on industry as well, such as the tariff.[51]

Advocates of democratic collectivism after the Civil War attempted to exploit these weaknesses in the agrarian creed. For example, they made a concerted attack on the very existence of natural rights, alleging their undemonstrability. And many of them remarked that even republicans had taken the right to property as conditional, given their support for state education, internal improvements at government expense, and the tariff, among other measures. Of course, they did not limit their criticism to such issues. Their ideology constituted a serious assault on the basic tenets of republicanism. Yet, a critique of the "decline" in the concept of individualism in the era following the Civil War must also take into account the obvious intellectual failures of liberals in that period. The votaries of constitutionalism contributed to the ultimate triumph of collectivism both by their inability to resolve the defects in republican theory and by their retreat from many of its most vital aspects.

CHAPTER II

THE FAILURE OF DEMOCRATIC LIBERALISM

The post–Civil War advocates of free government were the true heirs of the American revolutionaries. Like them, they championed the rights to both liberty and property, considerable freedom of enterprise, the participation of the people in the choosing of their rulers, and constitutionalism. They also took the individual as primary and distinguished between force and free association. Moreover, they, too, eschewed a pure laissez-faire policy, maintaining the necessity of providing through state action that milieu in which men could best exercise their abilities.

Still, these defenders of constitutional government played a role in the slow degeneration of individualism in the United States in the years following the Civil War. Although the collectivists forcefully assailed the limited state and undoubtedly greatly discredited it, it was in many ways the liberals themselves who helped most to bring about its downfall. In several respects, they abetted the victory of collectivism, for certain recurring weaknesses in their ideology worked to the advantage of their opponents. As a result, constitutional government perished more by intellectual default on the part of its proponents than by actual refutation.

Basically, democratic liberalism was beset by three main defects. First, it never came to grips with the problem of harmonizing the right to property with the existence of tax-supported service activities and restrictions on free trade, however minimal they may have been. This shortcoming opened supporters of free government to the charge that they were inconsistent and could not, therefore, oppose on grounds of principle projects that were patently designed to transfer property by law. Second, it was characterized by considerable ambiguity. Certain concepts were never defined. For instance, the "public interest" was used repeatedly, but its meaning was never particularized. Gradually, for many liberals, it came to connote a standard superior to individual rights, thereby relegating them to an ancillary status. Lastly, democratic liberalism was not defended on proper, theoretically rigorous grounds. The justifications adduced for it were never systematized into a coherent world view. They were often vague, philosophically inadequate, and subject to misinterpretation because of the imprecise or dubious use of words. Moreover, for various reasons, a comprehensive ethical code, which was desperately required, was not formulated. Indeed, not a few theorists came to accept more and more the ethical premises of their antagonists. In addition, crucial distinctions, upon which the case for constitutional government depended, were not always made clear or elaborated or even always maintained.

The intellectual luminaries of liberalism were those whose influence was exercised before 1900. Among them were Edwin Godkin, John Burgess, William Graham Sumner, Stephen Field, and certain free-market economists. Their successors were a great deal less liberal and even more antitheoretical. It is primarily the former who are here considered, for it was they who fought the battle against arbitrary government, and it was they who attempted a serious refutation of collectivism. Furthermore, they wrote in a period when neither educated nor public opinion had decided categorically between free government and collectivism, whereas at the time their successors took up the cudgels, the question had already been resolved in favor of the latter.

Advocates of the limited state argued that the essential choice which men had to make was between force and contract and that no third alternative existed. Once the principle that social forces could make rightful use of political organs for their own ends was accepted, they asserted, there would be no clear demarcation line by which the public could be set off from the private. Government would then be absolute in its powers, constrained only by considerations of general expediency. Thus, William Graham Sumner observed that if "we have been all wrong for the last three hundred years in aiming at a fuller realization of individual liberty, as a condition of general and widely-diffused happiness, then we must turn back to paternalism, discipline, and authority; but to have a combination of liberty and dependence is impossible." In remarking upon the income tax amendment, John Burgess noted that it gives Congress the power of confiscation, discriminates against the rich, and amounts to a redistribution of wealth by law. It results in putting all property, and therefore all human effort, at the mercy of the government, and it was a logical product of the prevailing tendency to sacrifice liberty to the organs of the state. Burgess readily drew the conclusion that the Sixteenth Amendment made "waste paper" of the Constitution, making it foolish for anyone to believe that "we have any longer a Constitution in regard to the relation between Government and the Individual in his rights to property or even to his own physical or mental efforts." Stephen J. Field, in commenting upon the decision of the Supreme Court in *Munn* v. *Illinois,* which acknowledged the right of the state legislature to fix the maximum rates for grain storage, wrote that Chief Justice Waite's doctrine of the public interest could be extended to the point where it would sanction the absolute control of the citizen by the state. The proposed legislation "is nothing less than a bold assertion of absolute power by the state to control at its discretion the property and business of the citizen, and fix the compensation he shall receive. The will of the legislature is made the condition upon which the owner shall receive the fruits of his property and the just rewards of his labor, industry and enterprise."[1] In general, liberals censured the protective tariff, the manipulation of the currency by the government, price-fixing by law, antitrust legislation, the creation of the Interstate Commerce Commission, and explicit redistribution of wealth by the public force.

Contrary to popular belief, however, they did not cling slavishly to laissez-faire. Post–Civil War liberals, like their republican predecessors, accorded a role to the state in fostering education and carrying out internal improvements. Many of them also recommended, albeit at the state level, aid to those who were physically incapable of supporting themselves, such as paupers, the disabled, and the insane. Others believed it was incumbent upon the government to enact factory legislation regulating the conditions of work. It would be an oversimplification to conclude that theirs was a philosophy of unmitigated laissez-faire.[2]

Just as with republican thinkers, these measures, especially education, were seen as providing a crucial environment for the maturation of individual talents and as redounding to the benefit, political and economic, of nearly all the people. In the form of aid to the incapacitated, they were also vindicated on humanitarian grounds. Yet, again the objection may be lodged that not all prospered in proportion to their pecuniary contribution and that some, indeed, did not profit at all. Surely, the intention was not to transfer wealth from one class to another, but the result may have indirectly led to that end. A major, lasting addition to the philosophy of free government would have involved the reconciliation of the right to property with these government projects, an exact determination of the boundary line between the national and state governments in the implementation of them (and a consideration of the attendant problem of "sovereignty"), and the evolving of a general theory of state functions. Nevertheless, despite their admonishments that the doom of liberty would follow the least acceptance of coercion for special purposes, exponents of constitutional government proved unwilling to address these issues in a satisfactory manner. They often denied that a problem existed at all, or they advanced cursory justifications that opened the path, paradoxically, to quite considerable political control of industry. Pertaining to the former, Sumner simply dismissed, without refuting, those reformers who wished to enlarge radically the sphere of "common" interests. "The fact that one thing has been given is made an argument for more. You are told: You have established free schools; 'why should not you' do whatever else the proponent favors? The argument that because you have given a man one thing you ought to give him another is not good in logic, but it is intensely strong in human nature and in history." With regard to the latter, Edwin Godkin maintained that the state should regulate gas and water works and transportation for essentially "utilitarian" reasons. "It makes no difference to me where I get my gas, or water, or transportation, provided I get it good and pure, provided I am not forced to take it if I do not want it, and provided I am not compelled to pay for anybody else's supply."[3] What he neglected to add was that if such were the case, government ownership of all industry in the country could be sanctioned on these grounds.

Those who espoused democratic collectivism exploited the

failure of the supporters of free government to present an adequate rationalization for these structural activities of the state. They contended that liberals were rebelling against logic by resisting on principle that extension of state power which would benefit certain groups directly and constitute an overt transfer of property by law. Justice Holmes, affirming in his dissent in *Lochner* v. *New York* that the majority had the right to embody its opinion in law, jibed that democratic liberals were blatantly contradictory in controverting on abstract grounds legislation that interfered with the individual's freedom of action. "The liberty of the citizen to do as he likes so long as he does not interfere with the liberty of others to do the same, which has been a shibboleth for some well-known writers, is interfered with by school laws, by the Post Office, by every state or municipal institution which takes his money for purposes thought desirable, whether he likes it or not." In the absence of a theoretical schema establishing the state's genuine functions and showing which powers were and which were not consonant with man's natural rights, liberals could not adequately reply to Holmes. In part, it was because their position appeared to be inconsistent that their influence steadily diminished throughout this period. Indeed, many of them seemed to relinquish in incremental steps their own basic viewpoint. As Richard Ely remarked as early as 1884, in the United States "it is curious to note how the advocates of *laissez faire* abandon position after position."[4] Unable to find a stable resting point, they often uncritically, and disastrously for their own cause, accepted state regulation in many areas, particularly under the pressure of popular clamor.

Proponents of limited government complicated matters by their inability to clarify the concept of the public interest. Indeed, they magnified its vagueness. They adduced no explicit definitions of it, although they alluded to it frequently.[5] For a goodly number, it did not denote a meaning as much as it symbolized a complex of sentiments thought to be desirable. At first, it was employed in a rather formal way to refer to legislation thought necessary by the canons of liberal political theory. Gradually, however, it began to acquire an additional connotation, that of a supraindividual standard by which the rights of individuals were to be gauged. Thus, in reviewing Edward Bellamy's *Looking Backward* (1888), the *Nation,* edited by Edwin Godkin, suggested that democracy "quite as much as Absolutism or Socialism recognizes the promotion of the public good as the basis of individual rights and the measure of individual duties." This concession negated the whole structure of the theory of rights by making them depend, not on the nature of the individual, but on the extent of his devotion to a public interest construed as service to others, exactly the position of the collectivists. John Burgess, more percipient in this regard, protested that the plea of the general welfare "always has been the broad avenue of approach to the inner temple of all liberty," but he also referred to, and at times justified freedom in terms of, the "highest welfare of the society and state."[6]

The pressure of the sequence of events after the Civil War made it imperative for democratic liberals to expurgate the ambiguities from their doctrines if they wished to preserve the limited state. The debunking of a mystical public interest would have been a valuable achievement in this context. Yet, by using the phrase rather loosely and by including practices under its rubric which seemed to many, including avowed collectivists, to be abridgments of the right to property, they weakened their own position. The common interest finally came to mean for some of them a standard which transcended individual rights and which was, in fact, the norm by which they were to be given content. In this respect, liberal political theory, as compared to republican individualism, effectively retrogressed, for republican thinkers had forthrightly discarded the idea that the general welfare either added to or detracted from man's right or that it conferred on government powers not enumerated in the Constitution. Supporters of limited government after the Civil War could have enlarged upon this conception and furnished a clear-cut definition of the "public good," thereby completely stripping it of all nebulousness. Defaulting on this responsibility and, indeed, adding to the confusion, they helped make possible its emergence as a tacit substitute for natural rights.

Most seriously of all, post–Civil War liberals were unable to present an internally consistent and intellectually satisfying defense of constitutional government. Now, this manifest flaw was not due to their alleged adoption of "evolutionism" as a basis for limited government, for the extent of Herbert Spencer's influence on serious political thought in America has been generally overestimated. Although they were conversant with his writings, the main thinkers, of whatever persuasion, did not rely upon him, John Fiske being the only significant exception. Those who upheld free government did bolster their position by citing his work and at times uttered the catchphrase "survival of the fittest." However, their essential views were in no way dependent upon the Spencerian philosophy, which was most usually invoked as an additional, scientific justification of liberal political theory.[7] Spencer made a much stronger impression among the popular adherents of the limited state and the industrialists, precisely those who were least familiar with republican tradition. Indeed, the long-range impact of Spencer's theories was such as to benefit the political cause he opposed. The collectivist terminology of his sociological works and his failure to indicate the standard by which fitness was to be judged made it possible for some of his political opponents to portray free exchange as the rule of the jungle, which it most emphatically was not, and for others to claim that the fittest were not surviving under such a system.

In any case, many of the deficiencies that eviscerated the arguments for free government are traceable to the philosophical void in which liberal intellectuals functioned. This explains the real origin of their unsystematic approach to political theory. Contemporaneous European liberalism was beset by the same problem, but unlike it, the American variety had been the foundation on which the nation was created and, not debauched by utilitarianism, had possessed the seeds of a philosophical doctrine in the concept of natural rights. The potential never became the actual, however, and liberals paid the appropriate price. Some of them rejected natural rights entirely, without providing a meaningful replacement; others accepted them uncritically, never striving to inquire into their raison d'être; still others blended them incongruously with other elements, creating intellectual befuddlement.[8]

Enunciating his beliefs in a vigorous and striking prose, Stephen Field was one of the few liberals of major stature who continued to insist upon the absolute validity of natural rights. Nevertheless, his legal opinions could not and did not provide any theoretical defense of such rights, confining themselves merely to the assertion of their existence, their application in a given case, and the deleterious effects that would result if a precedent were established for their violation. Because Field did not write any formal treatise, his imprint upon the course of thought was minor.[9]

John Burgess founded the Department of Political Science at Columbia University and exerted abundant influence, particularly upon law students; it cannot be said that this influence worked entirely in favor of liberalism. Burgess had studied in Germany and imbibed the terminology of German political theory, without absorbing its substance. Consequently, although he earnestly deplored the growth of the power of the state over individual citizens, his terminology was such as to bewilder his readers and to give them the impression that he idolized the state and set it above the individual. In his autobiography, he lamented that his critics misunderstood the meaning of his work, such men as Godkin, Garrison, and Villard representing it as the *Leviathan* of modern thought.[10]

Burgess shunned natural rights, perceiving them as "mere ideas which had gradually developed themselves in the minds of a given people." Apparently avowing the supremacy of some sort of collective, Burgess insisted that these ideas became rights only when they constituted "claims enforceable by organs empowered thereto by the state," and he further maintained that outside the state, the source of individual freedom, there "never was, and there never can be, any liberty upon this earth and among human beings." Incapable of limitation by either individual liberty or governmental power, the state could not be challenged.[11]

It is not surprising, then, that Burgess would be accused of setting the state apart from human purpose and endeavoring to make the citizens its slaves. However, although he cast aside natural rights, he did make a distinction between the state and the government. By the former, he simply meant the sovereign power, and when he said that the state could not be limited, he was making reference to the obvious fact that sovereignty was absolute and indivisible, that any attempt to constrain it would destroy it, and that the political decision-making power had to reside somewhere. As long as a state existed, it had to possess sovereignty, otherwise it was not truly a state. The government consisted of the organs of the state, the actual political machinery of the sovereign power. In the case of the United States, the

Constitution lay behind the government, and back of the Constitution was the "original sovereign state." Individual liberty and rights are not extirpated by the sovereign power; on the contrary, it is their only sound foundation and guaranty. The state restricts the government's authority in the interests of the liberty of the citizen and is in this sense the source of freedom. Political liberty can only be defined as the "absence of government in a given sphere of individual or social action."[12]

Nevertheless, the awkward terminology employed by Burgess and his occasional careless statements to the effect that the state could "do no wrong" made it easy for both friends and foes of limited government to interpret his thought as statist in its orientation.[13] Furthermore, the differentiation between the state and the government is hardly a basis on which to justify free government. Burgess's efforts in this regard are confined to historical appeals demonstrating the evils of governmental control and to the asseveration that freedom is required for both the highest development of the individual and the highest welfare of society. Broad declarations such as that modern political science "favors keeping open to private enterprise the widest possible domain of business" certainly did not set forth a systematic justification for freedom of enterprise or indicate its proper sphere.[14] Burgess, like Field, failed to give constitutional government a philosophical foundation, and moreover, his muddled phrasing and general remarks made it possible for his readers to misinterpret him.

The writings of Edwin Godkin were afflicted with a number of similar defects, and the *Nation*, during his editorship, faithfully reflected them. In many ways, Godkin is typical of the advocates of constitutionalism of this period. He aggressively attacked illiberal aspects of the political system immediately after the Civil War, and he gradually deserted this militancy over the years as he came to concede one collectivist assumption after another. He had a very great impact on the thought of his contemporaries, and the *Nation* was the recognized literary organ of the liberals. His writings mirrored the thinking of most partisans of free government, and simply for this reason, his great prestige aside, it is worthwhile to study them.

Godkin did not try to vindicate free government by any one norm but rather tended to uphold it by adducing both natural rights and utilitarian standards. When these were regarded as insufficient, he finally resorted to making an argument for the "survival of the fittest." What resulted was a very antisystematic, cracker-barrel approach to the great issues and problems of the day and an intellectual chaos perplexing to the rank-and-file of the liberal movement. When an undefined public interest was made to serve as a crowning conception, the befuddlement was complete.

None of the rationalizations offered by Godkin were clearly elaborated or expanded in a philosophical context, and one searches his writings in vain for a precise definition of terms. Furthermore, he seems to have burked any clear-cut consideration of the central issues that were being put forward by the collectivists. He himself had spoken, with regard to the inflation of the currency, of the distribution of wealth by political power and had condemned it as unjust.[15] Yet his desire to preserve certain measures of state interference without sanctioning them in theoretical terms even led him, at times, to deny the crucial distinction between governmental power and private agreement and to claim that the functions of the state were to be fixed purely by consulting experience. "Government," he wrote, "is from the outset, a joint-stock enterprise. To say that it may run a post-office, but must on no account carry on a gas-factory or water-works, would be absurd. But whether, besides running a post-office, it should also run gas-works and water-works depends on time and place and circumstances.[16]

When it came to appraising the effects of ethics on a man's actions and the part it should play, Godkin was rather vague. In his discussion of the "Economic Man," he apparently believed that economic action could take place without being regulated by ethical dicta. This is illustrated by his comment that moral criteria merely deflected the "Economic Man" from his normal course. Likewise, when he pondered the doctrine of self-interest, he was not able to arrive at any useful distinctions, apparently concluding only that plunder was to one's interest and that it was not practical from a long-range point of view.[17] He did not essay to develop an ethic which would furnish a firm prop for free government. As was true of other liberals, Godkin appeared to regard the introduction of ethical considerations as dangerous to the principle of free government and as somehow impermissible by scientific standards. When he exclaimed that there was no "absolute test of success in economic legislation" and that all the wise legislator could look forward to, given the complexity of the sociological problem, was the reduction in the amount of discontent among the poor, he was explicitly shirking the formulation of an axiological standard by which to ascertain what the state did owe, if anything, to its less fortunate citizens.[18] Godkin assuredly did not construct that conceptual base which democratic liberalism so sorely needed.

William Graham Sumner had substantial influence, although not as much as Godkin, and he was clearly the outstanding liberal of this period. Expressing himself in a blunt, pungent style, he was the most intransigent of the advocates of constitutional government, and he attempted, more so than other liberals, to provide both a coherent and moral refutation of collectivism. His analysis was acute and perceptive. He particularly excelled at exposing the hidden premises in collectivist excogitations and at showing what their actual results must be in practice, often illustrating his criticism by conjuring up vivid images, such as the "forgotten man." But Sumner's views suffered from a number of defects, and he, too, was unable to devise a throughgoing justification of limited government.

Although Sumner has been called the most influential social Darwinist in America during this period and has been depicted as having derived his main suppositions from Herbert Spencer,[19] he was definitely not a follower of Spencer. He did believe that Spencer had saved sociology from the "cranks," but he was far from approving of his work as a whole. The phrase "survival of the fittest" does appear in his essays, although not as often as might be supposed. Still, he did not use it in a purely adaptive sense. In almost all cases, he employed it as a synonym for liberty or as a description of the fact that in a free society, ability would be rewarded more than its lack.[20] The general format of a Spencerian analysis is completely missing from his political theory. Furthermore, from the standpoint of personal values, Sumner's intractable devotion to the work ethic and the spirit of Yankee enterprise made him incapable of attacking competition, no matter how severe, as Spencer did in his Farewell Address in 1882 in New York.[21]

Sumner's brand of liberalism was a mixture of hard common sense and self-interest interpreted as independence. It was vitiated, as was that of other liberals, by an imprecise use of terms, inconsistencies, and a variety of ambiguities. In Sumner's case, this was likely due almost entirely to his very strong antitheoretical bias. To it can be attributed his repugnance toward metaphysics and his contempt for the a priori speculations which were its product.[22] His aversion to theory made it possible for him to believe mistakenly that a comprehensive justification of free government, framed in philosophically rigorous terms, not only was not required but would in fact result in subverting it. Thus, Sumner wrote to David Wells, with reference to the majority decision in the case of *Loan Association* v. *Topeka,* that the "court has no right to bring in great *a priori* principles which underlie all free govts. This time it makes for us. Next time it will make for theirs [*sic*]."[23] This negative attitude toward abstract principles was the source of many of his difficulties.

The imprecision which characterizes Sumner's terminology is reflected in his usage of such phrases as "survival of the fittest" and in his treatment of such topics as natural rights and liberty. The meaning he imparted to the former has already been shown, but his definitions of the latter were likely to induce bewilderment. For instance, he defined liberty as power over nature. If this be true, then it is also true that a transfer of wealth from one class to another would increase the amount of freedom of the latter. Elsewhere, he made it clear that liberty under the law consists of securing to each man the use of all his powers for his own welfare and that the state cannot create freedom.[24] Yet, his occasional and reckless equation of liberty with the power to do conflicted with his more careful and elaborate statements on the matter.

Sumner's crusade against natural rights was also perplexing. In part, he rejected them because they were a priori abstractions held to be absolute. They could not be universally and timelessly true, because they were based on a doctrine. "A doctrine is an abstract principle; it is necessarily absolute in its scope and abstruse in its terms; it is a metaphysical assertion. It is never true, because it is absolute, and the affairs of men are all conditioned and relative."[25] Always present in his early writings, this relativistic view of rights was carried to an extreme in the seminal *Folkways* (1906).

Sumner denigrated natural rights as well because he accepted the collectivist concept that they were claims made on the

labor of others.[26] He does acknowledge that they were important in so far as they liberated men from social bonds and that
they were interpreted by many of the early American theorists
to mean the right to pursue a course of action, and not the right
to something, no matter how obtained.[27] If they are so interpreted, then we do indeed have them. "We each owe it to the
other to guarantee rights. Rights do not pertain to *results*, but
only to chances. They pertain to the *conditions* of the struggle
for existence, not to any of the results of it; to the *pursuit* of
happiness, not to the possession of happiness."[28] Nevertheless,
Sumner seldom made this point clear and continued to declaim
against natural rights as a species of dogmatism. This had the
baneful result of making him appear as an enemy of human
rights per se, one who was legitimizing the trampling down of
the weak by the strong by establishing no ethical standards of
conduct save that of the "survival of the fittest." It also placed
him outside, although only apparently, the mainstream of
American political thought, something his critics could not
have done on their own. Even today, most of the assessments of
his work do not take into account the qualifications that he
affixed to his gainsaying of the theory of natural rights.[29]

Just as with John Burgess, once the doctrine of natural rights
was rejected, constitutional government was left hanging in the
air, unsupported by any convincing arguments. It would be
foolish to say that a simple restatement of this thesis would have
made Sumner's position impregnable, but the espousal of it
and the deduction from it of unambiguous conclusions most
likely would have eliminated the contradictions and vagueness
that marked his views. However, only a serious inquiry into the
ground of natural rights would have put an obstacle into the
way of collectivism; the mere affirming of their reality would
not and did not during this period. When Sumner lambasted
theory, he effectively discarded the possibility of justifying
constitutional government in sweeping terms devoid of all
nebulousness. Consequently, it is hard to distill from his
writings any coherent justification at all.

To defend free government, Sumner apparently thought it
quite sufficient to call the attention of its antagonists to a
number of facts. For instance, he stated that the government
can not get wealth for some men without taking it away from
others, that all historical experience is against state regulation

and in favor of liberty, that constitutional government secures rights and adjusts the collision of interests, that individual initiative and private property are the bedrock of civilization, that liberty has been achieved only where barriers are set up to class rule, and that paternalism leads inexorably to regulation.[30] Such facts, moral implications aside, and the assumptions on which they were based were exactly those in dispute. Sumner appears to have taken it for granted that no extensive discussion was required to prove that the state was no more than the sum of its citizens, that wealth had to be produced and was not a static quantity, and that political power was qualitatively different from economic power. He, therefore, did not expatiate upon these and other topics and give them the clarification they deserved. Needless to say, such a failure worked to the advantage of his opponents, who were not lacking loquacity when it came to such matters.

Concerning ethics, two main lines of thought are to be found in Sumner's writings, and neither one was ever reconciled with the other. One tendency was to provide a quasi-ethical refutation of ethics, and the other was to get away from moral issues altogether by minimizing the role values played in human action. Although both tendencies are to be found throughout his writings, the latter is clearly predominant in his later work, particularly *Folkways*.

Sumner, unlike Godkin and many other liberals, even those who supposedly adhered to a natural rights position, never displayed the least sympathy for altruism, nor did he think that the legislator should act so as to benefit any special class of persons. The altruistic justification for free production never found a place in his theories. On the contrary, those precepts which Sumner enumerated are all founded on the fundamental duty of the individual to support himself through his own efforts; charity is largely relegated to the domain of private relations and even then not to be given indiscriminately. Free men in a constitutional republic owe each other only "goodwill, mutual respect and mutual guarantees of liberty and security." Because morality presupposes choice, Sumner is affirming volition by positing ethical rules, and he notes that the greatest reforms would consist in undoing much of the work of the statesmen of the past. To the legions of "social quacks," he replies that it no doubt wounds the vanity of a philosopher who is just ready with a new solution of the universe to be told to mind his own business. So he goes on to tell us that if we think that we shall, by being let alone, attain a perfect happiness on earth, we are mistaken. The half-way men—the professorial socialists—join him. They solemnly shake their heads, and tell us that he is right—that letting us alone will never secure us perfect happiness. Under all this lies the familiar logical fallacy, never expressed, but really the point of the whole, that we *shall* get perfect happiness if we put ourselves in the hands of the world-reformer. We never supposed that *laissez faire* would give us perfect happiness. We have left perfect happiness entirely out of our account. If the social doctors will mind their own business, we shall have no troubles but what belong to Nature. Those we will endure or combat as we can. What we desire is, that the friends of humanity should cease to add to them.[31]

Although Sumner avoided the apologetics of other liberals and came closer than any other major theorist of liberalism to an appreciation of the axiological bases indispensable to a rigorous defense of constitutional government, his general propensity was to shy away from the formulation of a systematic theory of ethics. Basically, this deficiency stemmed from the preemption of the sphere of morality by altruism, which made it difficult for him, or for anyone else, to propose any contrary axiology. Sumner clearly identified the public interest, in its negative connotation, with altruism and tended to equate the latter to the "ought" in general, as demonstrated in his comment that socialistic doctrines always labor to justify the enslavement of some men by others by invoking the "ought."[32] His suspicion of the "ought" was, by and large, grounded in the fact that he construed it as a coercive dictate, the means by which some people ruled the lives of others. Consequently, he denied that there could be any injunctions in political economy and righteously and repeatedly declaimed against the authority of abstract ethical standards and the meddling of social philosophers. Yet, often preceding or following such declarations he set forth what men did, in fact, owe each other.[33] Paradoxically, Sumner's war against morality was inspired by moral indignation and couched in highly moralistic terms. Unfortunately, it not only prevented him from devising a well-elaborated theory of obligation but resulted as well in an intellectual confusion benefited the cause of collectivism, which, whatever its merits, did have a moral theory. Sumner's fatal error here was to suppose that an order of freedom would not require a deontology or that practical maxims would somehow do. Even the courageous and frank *What Social Classes Owe to Each Other* (1883), which might have served as a propaedeutic for a sophisticated treatment of the moral bases of liberalism, was marred by these suppositions.

To make matters worse and compound the chaos, another tendency could also be extracted from Sumner's writings, to wit, the attempt to belittle the role of moral values in human action, in the apparent expectation, or hope, that their denigration as causal factors would eliminate the fundamental ethical props upon which socialists and reformers had erected their arguments. This predilection conveys Sumner to a personally uncharacteristic apology for social and political quiescence and a quasi-determinism. He deprecates ideals as "vague and inconclusive generalizations," unscientific and having no connection with the facts. Indeed, if ideals are precisely that with which ethics deals, then it is entailed that on "every ground and at every point the domain of social science must be defended against the alleged authority of ethical dicta, which cannot be subjected to any verification whatever." Unfortunately, Sumner noted, the tradition of philosophy made it respectable to judge social organization by axiological standards. But the power of ideas is a myth; ideals, ethics, and philosophy are all secondary and arise out of the mores, although reciprocal interaction may occur.[34] There can be no question that the folkways "are not creations of human purpose and wit. They are like products of natural forces which men unconsciously set in operation, or they are like the instinctive ways of animals, which are developed out of experience, which reach a final form of maximum adaptation to an interest, which are handed down by tradition and admit of no exception or variation, yet change to meet new conditions, still within the same limited methods, and without rational reflection or purpose."[35]

Sumner was inevitably led by this line of reasoning to adopt an extremely relativistic view of rights, thereby weakening what he sought to defend, for if rights are derived from the folkways and the latter are constantly changing to adapt themselves to interests, then they cannot be absolute and are at any time a social product, not abstractions by which government must be limited. Rights are simply the "rules of the game" and do not exist antecedent to civilization. " 'Rights' are the rules of mutual give and take in the competition of life which are imposed on comrades in the in-group, in order that the peace may prevail there which is essential to the group strength. Therefore rights can never be 'natural' or 'God-given,' or absolute in any sense. The morality of a group at a time is the sum of the taboos and prescriptions in the folkways by which right conduct is defined. Therefore morals can never be intuitive. They are historical, institutional, and empirical."[36] Sumner finally arrived at a conservatism which focused on continuity and the futility of human reason to appraise social arrangements and to alter the world, making change independent of human effort.[37]

The tragedy of democratic liberalism in America was that a movement originated by men who had full confidence in the rectitude of their cause and who were willing to break with the past, risking their lives and fortunes to "make the world over," was ultimately transformed into a rather anti-intellectualistic reaction against change as such. Certainly, the American creed of individualism had not been based on uncritical worship of tradition or on the despair that human reason was incapable of apprehending and changing reality. Defending it in such terms not only failed to prevent its downfall but was an essential betrayal of its spirit.

By the turn of the century, liberalism as an effective force had perished. All the political parties conceded, to a greater or lesser degree, the precept that the state enjoyed broad powers founded on an undefined public good. The intellectual trend was manifestly against limited government, and by the time of the 1912 presidential election it had become apparent that a true exponent of free government could not support any of the parties and that the point of no return had passed. Liberals such as John Burgess were well aware of what had happened.

The Jingo and the Social Reformer have gotten together and have formed a political party, which threatened to capture the Government and use it for the realization of their programme of Caesaristic paternalism, a danger which appears now to have been averted only by the other parties having themselves adopted this programme in a somewhat milder degree and form. All parties are now declaring themselves to be Progressives, and all mean in substance the same thing by this claim, viz: the increase of governmental power over the constitutional Immunities of the Individual, the solution by force of the problems of the social relations heretofore regulated by influence, by religion, conscience, charity, and human feeling, the substitution of the club of the policeman for the crosier of the priest, the supersession of education, morals, and philanthropy by administrative ordinance.[38]

The new generation of democratic liberals not only were unable to resolve the difficulties that had been bequeathed them by their mentors but seemed to augment them, making concessions that would have been branded as "socialistic" earlier in the period. Their political philosophy was distinguished by a solidly antitheoretical view of state functions, an emphasis on tradition and the dangers of innovation, and a depreciation of moral egoism as a basis for free government.

Generally speaking, they sought some form of compromise between freedom of production and exchange and a broad regulation of industry. Their advocacy of such a solution was made possible only by the acceptance, to at least some degree, of many of the collectivist tenets, by the minimizing, annulling, or, most usually, the evading of certain distinctions that the previous generation of liberals had thought crucial. Thus, Elihu Root could say, without adducing proof, that in the age of combinations, contract was no longer free and that men who headed trusts were getting more than their "fair share." Governmental interference with free choice was consequently necessary to preserve freedom. William Howard Taft supported regulation of the trusts, maintaining that they can coerce, the tariff, and a variety of measures directed against "unfair" practices and the "suppression" of competition. Sociologist Franklin Giddings thought that the trusts had been unjustly maligned, but he did favor extensive and undefined governmental regulation of business and, like the others, grounded his position in expediency. "Thus," he wrote, "it will be seen that the question of expediency is one not at all likely to be answered *a priori* or conformably to any preconceived theory. It will be answered only after much experience, only by much experiment, only through a great multitude of tentative rules and decisions."[39]

In all these instances, liberals denied the distinction between coercion and free choice, either implicitly or explicitly, and like the collectivists, they reached the conclusion that force could create freedom. But unlike their opponents, they insisted upon restricting the sphere of state intervention as much as possible. Thus, after acknowledging the need for state action, they affirmed that governmental controls should not be exercised recklessly and that the individual's rights to liberty and property should be reorganized as the foundation of American civilization.[40] Yet the problem in determining the limits of state power was not that the "test" was "difficult of application," as Elihu Root asserted.[41] Rather, because there was no kind of objective standard by which to ascertain where force ended and freedom began, a strong tendency existed to accept many measures of state interference without adequate proof that they were necessary or constitutional or compatible with human rights.

More telling in the decline of liberalism was its lack of moral fervor and its practically complete acknowledgment of altruism as a desirable goal. There was a great deal of discussion of the rights of the workingmen and poor, but little talk of those of the employers, save in so far as they were construed as the "privilege" to serve the community. It was pointed out that the exaggerations of individualism offered a legitimate field for socialist criticism and that the socialists did "admirable" work in certain areas. The motives of both socialists and individualists were fathomed to be the same, for "the point of issue between individualism and socialism is not a question of ends, but of means. Both sides have the same object at heart, namely, the general good of society."[42] Root affirmed that the central force of progress had been selfishness and that the "noble" standards of altruism and human sympathy must await the millenium for their complete fulfillment. Because human nature and consequently government are imperfect, to enforce such standards by law would be impossible. In other words, if it were not for human depravity, there would be no objection in principle to a compulsory direction of man's labor for "desirable" ends. The adoption of "social morality" is also seen in the writings of Giddings, who made the "feeling of kind" the keystone of his sociology and spoke of increasing the workers' control over the products and conditions of industry. And William Howard Taft commented favorably on the fact that from 1900 to 1905 workingmen obtained a greater percentage of the industrial product and managers less.[43] Other liberals made remarks to the same effect.

The intellectual and moral position at which liberalism finally arrived is epitomized by the introductions that a number of prominent figures appended to the various chapters of Spencer's *Man versus the State,* published in a new American edition in 1916. The contributors included such notables as Root, Taft, Henry Cabot Lodge, and Nicholas Murray Butler.[44] None of these men were willing to go as far as Spencer in their condemnation of state action, citing him only as a warning. What they bewailed was not the extensive and arbitrary state interference that had occurred before World War I but "over-legislation" or doing "too much" in the present and the future. However, they never stated the standard by which legislation is to be adjudged as supernumerary. They made absolutely no effort to set forth a consistent political philosophy or to examine problems in terms of broad essentials. Consequently, the basic assumptions in the arguments of the reformers are either implicitly conceded or simply burked. This is particularly true with regard to the moral issues. What impresses one most in reading these essays is, given the nature of the early revolutionary republicanism, their self-effacing style and utter lack of any crusading spirit. Liberalism had been fully transformed into a nonintellectual hodgepodge intended to moderate and slow down the rate of change, but not advancing any fundamental objections to the policies of statism.

In conclusion, those who took up the cause of free government during this period were wont to treat it as a finished product, fundamentally sound and in need of no extensive development or revision. Its maxims, they felt, had only to be applied to concrete situations, and all would be well. Their antagonists, however, were by no means of the opinion that their position was invincible. They pointed to the apparent inconsistencies and obvious ambiguities present in the doctrines of those who endorsed limited, constitutional government. They also noted, and took advantage of, the failure of democratic liberals to produce a systematic and moral justification for their convictions. Instead of regarding the criticism of reformers as a challenge to clarify, refine, and elaborate their beliefs into an intelligible whole, those who advocated free government shied away from political theory proper and even constitutional exegesis, retreating into meaningless compromise or even adopting, though largely implicitly, some of the tenets of their critics. They ignored Madison's call for a comprehensive theory which would reveal what exceptions to free trade were permissible, and they did not attempt to discover which service activities, if any, were to be performed by government and how they were to be harmonized with property rights. Hence, they were unable to define lucidly the boundary line between the public and the private (and thus give concrete content to the public interest) and to ascertain whether or not state action in a given case was appropriate. A reconsideration of such issues as consent, sovereignty, and the taxing power and a detailed analysis of the concepts of contract, property, rights, and force might have served to reinvigorate individualist doctrine, freeing it from vagueness and seeming contradictions. Without this theoretical and necessary development, free government became all the more vulnerable to the cutting attack launched against it by its foes, one which drastically transformed the republican conception of individualism.

CHAPTER III

THE REIFICATION OF SOCIETY

Many progressives after the Civil War essayed to portray their ideology as constituting a new and higher form of individualism. Whether or not this assertion is correct, their understanding of individualism was radically different from that of the Founding Fathers; a continuity between the two can be presumed only by taking words at their face value and ignoring their conceptual referents. The main reform movements of the latter half of the nineteenth and the early part of the twentieth century did not protest in the name of limited government, however much they wished to retain the label of individualism. They sought active state intervention, borrowing not from the liberal heritage but from the Fabian socialists and Bismarckian Germany, as Arthur Ekirch has noted. Indeed, as he has pointed out, "from the perspective of a later age it is possible to see that the progressives were essentially nationalists, moving to a state socialism along European lines and owing relatively little to the American tradition of liberal individualism."[1]

One major and crucial difference between the republican idea of individualism and that of the collectivist-oriented intellectuals of the post–Civil War period does not consist in substantive political issues relating to the origin and proper scope of the state as such. Rather, it resides in key metaphysical distinctions. Republicans perceived the political order as subservient to the interests of the autonomous individual and posited both society and state as products of the association of metaphysically independent men. They explicitly rejected the belief that the whole was something greater than its parts. The advocates of the "positive" state, however, started from the assumption that society was something other than an aggregation of individuals. Indeed, most of them expounded that the individual was an abstraction and that society (or the state or the nation) was a real entity. Consequently, thinking a collective to be existentially superior to the individuals who compose it, they held that the ultimate object of inquiry was not the individual but a discarnate public, and this latter was to be the subject of analysis. Once society had been studied, then knowledge of individuals could be obtained. Thus, the method of the collectivists was the diametrical opposite of that of the republicans, for the latter started with the individual and took society to be a derivative product.

The writings of the prominent intellectuals of this period, with the exception of the dwindling band of democratic liberals, reveal the disrepute into which the "abstract" individual had fallen, with the concomitant elevation of society. Over and over again, the term "society" was used as if it were a physical being and political questions were discussed in terms of whether a given policy would conduce to the benefit of society. Individuals were usually introduced into the discussion in a rather casual and secondary manner. Quite naturally, this reification of society gave rise to the concept of a supraindividual public interest, which became the yardstick by which all issues were to be adjudged.

It may be objected that those reformers who emphasized the importance of the group did not reify society. Arthur Bentley, for instance, sometimes seemed to deny that the general welfare was a valid concept, yet many of the group theorists did use the term "society" rather promiscuously and in a collectivistic way. In their thought, although the public good emerged on a different level, it was nevertheless there, and it certainly did not denote the mere securing of natural rights. Most group theorists, in fact, abjured the existence of the abstract individual, reified the group, and then proceeded to sanction group interaction by maintaining that it was in the public good, which was still regarded as something other than a convenient symbol for individual rights or even group interplay.

Political theory is dependent upon ethics, which, in turn, is ultimately dependent upon metaphysics and epistemology. The positing of society as a physical existent made possible the specific political prescriptions advanced by collectivist intellectuals and in this sense constituted their fundamental premise. As such, it was implied in all their reasoning and was a necessary prerequisite for demonstrating that the role of the state should be arbitrarily expanded. It was upon metaphysical collectivism that both ethical and political collectivism were erected.[2] The reification of society played a most crucial part in diverting attention away from the individual actor and the conditions necessary for his welfare. In effect, reformers removed the individual from their version of individualism. The arguments designed to prove the overall desirability of a collectivist order centered on the injustices done to society under the existing system of constitutional government, and from these injustices wrongs allegedly committed against individuals were deduced. To be sure, the conception of society as entity was not always explicitly introduced in the criticisms made of free government, and deductions were seldom rigorously made in the sense of one premise following logically from another until the desired conclusion was obtained. Still, the tacit assumption that society was more than those who comprised it was always present and served an indispensable function in the construction of the argument.

Even the pragmatists, despite their disdain for absolutes, did not by any means reject societal collectivism. They may have dethroned the otherworldly form of collectivism, but they did not exalt the individual, nor did they crush all idols. From the beginning, pragmatism was endowed with a community orientation. Charles Peirce, regarded as the founder of pragmatism, offered two definitions of truth. The first stated that reality was independent of what any man or group of men might think, whereas the second considered truth to be the "opinion which is fated to be ultimately agreed to by all who investigate." Peirce engaged in rather crude mental gymnastics to demonstrate that the two definitions were compatible, yet it is clear that they are not, and he tended to adhere to the second rather than the first. In fact, his main statement attempting to reconcile the two definitions actually simply reaffirmed the second. "But the reality of that which is real does depend on the real fact that investigation is destined to lead, at last, if continued long enough, to a belief in it."[3] Thus, Peirce offered a subjectivist definition of truth, one which made reality dependent on the mind of the observer. Most importantly, however, he collectivized truth as well. Reality became a function of the collective beliefs of a community of investigators, not something to be apprehended by the individual consciousness. This collectivist epistemological approach of pragmatism was totally in harmony with the period's emphasis on society, and it was taken up by most pragmatists, especially under the influence of John Dewey.[4]

The early works in the post–Civil War period that attained a certain degree of influence over the development of American political thought were not marked by any serious, detailed criticism of free government. But such books as Orestes Brownson's *The American Republic* (1865) and Elisha Mulford's *The Nation* (1870) did have an impact on the intellectual course of events and did provide the initial impetus in altering the focus of study from the individual to society. Brownson and Mulford were rather vague when it came down to adducing specific prescriptions for change, and they were not as empirically oriented as later theorists. Still, they helped make it respectable, intellectually speaking, to deny the supposed eternal verities, such as the metaphysical priority of the individual, consent as the basis of government, rights as predicated of isolated individuals, and what may best be termed "legalism." Their religious tone, however, was increasingly out of place in an increasingly secular age, and this aspect of their thought was by and large spurned by the great majority of intellectuals who followed them. Nevertheless, the political conclusions that ineluctably stem from the assertion of a metaphysical collectivism were drawn by succeeding theorists.

Mulford derided that conception which would base the state upon pallid abstractions, such as natural rights, and make it the product of conscious choice. The nation was not simply a composite wrought by artifice; it was an organism in the full sense of the word. Generally, his analysis was cast in Hegelian terms, and he tended to equate the state to the nation. Brownson made repeated avowals that the victory of the North in the Civil War should not be interpreted as a triumph for the "socialistic" opinions of the abolitionists and humanitarians who would dissolve the individual in the race and exalt the people as God. His objection, if taken at face value, is curious in that he continually reified society and counterposed it to the abstract individual who supposedly has no real existence. He frankly stated that society can be understood without any reference whatsoever to the individual. "Society, and government as representing society, has a real existence, life, faculties, and organs of its own, not derived or derivable from individuals." Thus, he was quick to cast aside the social contract and all that it implied, for it signified a purely mechanical, soulless unity and did not take into account the fact that society is not an artificial construction. "Society is not an aggregation, nor even an organization of individuals. It is an organism, and individuals live in its life as well as it in theirs. There is a real living solidarity, which makes individuals members of the social body, and members one of another. . . . in society, there is that which is not individual, and is more than all individuals. . . . Real government has its ground in this real living solidarity, and represents the social element, which is not individual, but above all individuals." The purpose of government was to render the nation an organism, not a mere collocation of citizens, and its function was therefore positive as well as negative. But other than stating that individual liberty should be utilized for the common weal, Brownson did not expressly draw the political consequences of his reification of society. He seemed satisfied just with proving that the individual is to be subordinated to the collective, metaphysically and morally, and that society can not be understood as a product of the interactions of individuals.[5]

This holistic conception was present in the writings of most intellectuals in this period, being advanced most strenuously by sociologists. From the metaphysical standpoint, however, nothing essentially new was added to the ruminations of Brownson and Mulford, except for the empirical concern with groups. No credible proofs were proffered that demonstrated that individual existence was a myth and society a reality. Those who followed Brownson and Mulford did little more than reiterate the theme that the individual was an abstraction when separated from society.

There was some dispute as to whether society or the state constituted an organism. For instance, Henry Jones Ford, writing in 1915, noted that the organic theory of the state had declined in influence among political theorists, although he preferred to accept it as his standpoint, claiming that sociologists had accepted it to a greater degree. He depicted the state as an organism, capable of being "defined as an organic entity composed of human beings whose nature, relations and activities are conditioned by its own nature, relations and activities." Yet he also maintained that man was a social product. Other writers criticized the reification of the state. For instance, James W. Garner ridiculed it as "fanciful and absurd," and Harry

Elmer Barnes observed, at the end of this period, that *contra* Ford, the biological school of sociologists had become one of the least important.[6] The differences between the two positions, nevertheless, were more apparent than real. Those theorists who did reify the state, like Ford, generally were quite willing to assert, as did he, that man was a "social product." When they affirmed that the state was organic, they meant only that the web of relationships in which men found themselves was more than the sum of individual actions. The state was organic in that it embodied certain of these relationships, namely, those pertaining to the political element, but this did not imply that society was not organic. As with Mulford, those who hypostatized the state usually reified society as well,[7] although they were often ambiguous as to the exact relation between the two.

Adopting and elaborating the outlook of Brownson and Mulford, the American brand of collectivism, then, took society as the motor and real subject of change and alleged its existence qua physical entity. Throughout the literature of this period, one finds recurrent statements of this view, so that at the end of it, it is regarded a commonplace, hardly worth debating. Woodrow Wilson concluded, in his work *The State* (1889), that society is to be conceived of as an organism and government as its primary instrument. Eminent economist John Bates Clark cited the "discovery of recent times that a society is not merely like an organism; it is one in literal fact." Henry Carter Adams, in his very influential *The Relation of the State to Industrial Action* (1887), shunned as the subject of investigation both the individual and the state, perceiving society as "the organic entity about which all our reasoning should center." Walter Weyl, a thoroughgoing pragmatist who emphasized the role of groups in the socialization of industry, commented that "no democracy is possible in America except a socialized democracy, which conceives of society as a whole and not as a more or less adventitious assemblage of myriads of individuals." Muckraking journalist Henry Demarest Lloyd indicated that those who reduced the study of mankind to the relations existing among individual men were gravely in error. "But there is a people," he proclaimed, "and it is as different from a mere juxtaposition of persons as a globe of glass from the handful of sand out of which it was melted." Herbert Croly took to task those whose thought was "dominated by the illusion of physical individuality" for assuming the existence of separate individuals merely from "certain physical symptoms." Lamenting that these unfortunates "never recognized the existence of sociality as a primary psychological fact," he believed that society should be "conceived as a whole, with certain paramount interests and needs, into which the different centres of association must be fitted."[8] Innumerable other theorists such as Edward Bellamy, Thorstein Veblen, and James Allen Smith expressed similar ideas. Still others, while not troubling themselves to author dicta to the effect that society was an entity, simply presumed that it was and made their whole chain of reasoning dependent upon this presumption.

In this regard, the writings of Henry George and Lester Ward are of great moment. Both contributed substantially to the collectivist movement, although each in somewhat different ways. Henry George continually bandied about the term "society," treating it as if it were a real existent. Despite his claim to be an advocate of natural rights, he frequently personified society and made constant reference to the functions it would assume in the future and the benefits it would confer on the human race. And his scheme, of course, involved the societal ownership of land to be achieved by confiscation of rent. George's primary importance lies, as some observers have realized, not in his particular solution for the curing of society's ills but in his appeal to malcontents of all kinds, which made criticism of the existing order seem legitimate and accelerated the development of collectivism in America by stressing the paramountcy of society.[9] Making it fashionable to think in terms of the collective and not the individual, George had an especially great influence over the popular mind. "George's great contribution was perhaps neither his panacea nor his specific analysis, but rather his vivid presentation of his belief that the material progress of society was the outcome of the growth of society, that the greatest gains had come to the possessors of strategic resources, rendered valuable by the progress of society, not by the contributions of the possessors."[10] Even if one were to grant the validity of the accusation that owners of land financially benefited from the general increase of business in a community without playing any constructive part in bringing it about and that, therefore, they should not profit from it, it would still not follow that society, or the state acting in its name, should confiscate rent. On the contrary, as one critic has pointed out, all that could be established would be the right of each man to his "aliquot part of the site value of every plot of land—*not* the *state's* right to the whole value."[11] It was George's glorification of society that led him to a proposal which did not follow, strictly speaking, from his premises.

If collectivism first reached a large audience through the vehicle of Henry George's writings, it remained for a more profound thinker to give it a systematic basis. Lester Ward, who became in 1906 the first president of the American Sociological Association, can probably be considered as the major intellectual critic of free government in this period. He exerted more influence than is commonly supposed, particularly on the rising generation of scholars, and he had a telling effect on the evolution of sociological theory in America. He not only reified society; he also drew the appropriate conclusions from his metaphysical presumptions. He expressed more systematically and more persistently than did Brownson and Mulford the view that society could not be considered as a product of individual wills. He paved the way as well for later theorists who would focus upon the group at the expense of the individual, although little outright group analysis is to be found in his writings.

Ward held that society was primary and that the state had one mission: the securing of the welfare of society. Evolutionary theory as Ward understood it did not dictate that the status quo was sacred, for the appearance of consciousness on the scene meant that the environment could be intelligently transformed; the political system was subject to volition. Additionally, however, volition, interests, intellect, and will could be truly predicated of society, which alone, using to best advantage its collective mind, could solve the problems confronting mankind. What formerly had been attributed to the individual was now regarded as the property of society, and Ward frankly urged that society discard the anachronistic laissez-faire philosophy and deal with its own affairs in its own way. "The individual has reigned long enough. The day has come for society to take its affairs into its own hands and shape its own destinies." It was this concept of the community which made it possible for Ward to assert that it had problems not explicable or solvable in individualistic terms. In an eloquent passage reifying society, he made it clear that it was exactly analogous to an individual, except that it was an organism of a superior order, and that it should act in its own interests, employing collective telesis.

The individual has grappled with physical forces and with psychic forces and has laid them tribute to his will. It remains for society in its collective capacity to grapple with the social forces and to render them in like manner subject to the social will. But to do this society must wake to consciousness even as the individual has done. It must develop a social intellect capable of exercising both the forms of indirection described. Society must become cunning, shrewd, strategic and diplomatic in compassing its own interests, but especially it must acquire ingenuity and inventiveness in dealing with the heterogeneous mass of human beings out of which it is constituted, all of whom, however, are actuated in every movement by fixed laws that it must first discover. The social intellect must imitate in all respects the individual intellect. It must even be egoistic, since its own interests are also those of its individual components, and therefore there is no possibility of injury except through failure to secure those interests.[12]

Ward's epistemological and metaphysical collectivism was consistent and complete, and he greatly developed an idea which had remained implicit and rudimentary in the writings of his predecessors: the role of the collective mind in directing the social organism. Ward never specified precisely which groups were qualified to speak in the name of the social intellect, but he definitely did insinuate that intellectuals, most especially sociologists imbued with the collectivist and scientific spirit and versed in the arcane ways of the social forces, would exercise this function. In any case, he evinced a powerful distrust of the individual mind and private judgment, as did a great many intellectual reformers in the post–Civil War era, and his collectivization of intelligence was a manifestation of this distrust. "Such a powerful weapon as reason is unsafe in the hands of one individual when wielded against another. It is still more dangerous in the hands of corporations, which proverbially have no souls. . . . It is only safe when employed by the social ego, emanating from the collective brain of society, and directed toward securing the common interests of the social organism."[13] The progressives who succeeded Ward operated within the framework he had helped to build. They thought and wrote in terms of a social or public interest not derivable from the nature of the individual and capable of being ascribed only of a supraindividual society, whose existence became the self-evident premise of their theories. With Ward, they believed that the individual had ruled long enough and that it was time for society to take control. When they expatiated upon the social forces whose existence Ward had revealed, they found them to reside in groups. This infatuation with the group in no way implied that man was not a social product or that society was not an entity, for it merely added an "empirical" element, albeit an important one, which had been lacking in certain writers, such as Brownson and Mulford, but intimated in others, such as Ward. Those who reified the group were almost always prone to reify society as well and usually, although tacitly, regarded the former as a constituent part of the latter.[14]

Arthur Bentley did discourse that the concept of the social whole was vague and that society was only the arena in which groups contended.[15] He often used the word "society" in a collectivistic sense, however, and it is difficult to see how a pluralist theorist can really avoid the concept of a public interest (collectivistically construed). For it would seem absurd to propound that if the group were the sole entity, a man could be part of more than one entity at the same time, or if he joined some new groups and deserted others, that he could voluntarily choose to detach himself from one body and then attach himself to another. Furthermore, for a variety of reasons, it became imperative to denote the final result reached by the process of group interaction as being in society's interest, the criterion by which policy was to be judged. Consequently, it is not astonishing that most group theorists, at least in this period, tended to visualize the group as a sort of subordinate entity, an empirical reference point which greatly assisted the investigator in studying the motions in the social whole, and not as something independent of society.

Particularly, in Bentley's case, one can argue that his basic assumptions easily gave rise to the notion of a public interest superseding individuals and groups. For, if it is averred, as Bentley did, that we know men only by their relations to each other, by their social activity,[16] and that entities, in this case groups, are posited where patterns of such activity are discerned, then it is also true that interactions among such groups constitute a pattern of a distinctive sort and that "society as a whole" is that pattern.

Those who stressed the group agreed with Bentley that it was the social element which defined man, and not vice versa. They disclaimed that man was an isolated causal agent who determined his own actions, for "there is no idea which is not a reflection of social activity. There is no feeling which the individual can fix upon except in a social form. He can define it only in terms of language which myriads of men have built up. He knows what he feels, and indeed even that he feels, only in terms of other men's lives."[17] This theme had become a trite one by the beginning of World War I, and most writers on politics adopted it without reserve. The conception of the group as an essential part of an integral society supplanted the idea of the individual as an independent entity freely determining his own destiny. Thus, Harry Elmer Barnes, who studied carefully the nature and extent of the impact of sociology on political theorizing in this period, discerned that the social determination of political thought had been conceded and that most sociologists agreed that the adjustment of group interests was the foremost process of government. He observed further, and with evident approval, that no "such thing as the abstract isolated individual is known to social science" and in confirmation of the previous analysis of Bentley's pluralism, he found his emphasis on group interaction totally compatible with references to the "social organism as a whole." James W. Garner's *Introduction to Political Science*, written in 1910 and designed to serve as a textbook transmitting the discoveries of scholars to students, reveals the extent to which the individual had been displaced from the center of analysis. Garner expostulated that individualists "overemphasize the importance of the man at the expense of the group; they treat him as if he were paramount and as if he determined the character of society when in fact it is society, as has been said, that determines in a large degree the character of the individual." Numerous utterances to the same end can be found in practically all the major works on politics from 1900 onwards, and where they cannot be found, the subjection of the individual to the group (within the societal context) is usually assumed as a metaphysical axiom. Albion Small, disciple and admirer of

Lester Ward and a leading sociologist in his own right, perspicaciously wrote in 1916: "Perhaps the most familiar illustration of the sort of change referred to . . . is the revolution which has taken place within the last twenty-five years, in all thinking about human experience, through shifting the emphasis from the assumed individual agent to the *group* in which persons are now seen to be subordinate factors."[18]

The reification of society was a crucial supposition in the theories of progressives, and it was implicit in practically every theorem they advanced to justify the collectivist state. Its importance can hardly be overestimated. But it was more directly employed in certain arguments than in others, and it would not be fruitless to examine here one of these arguments in particular, showing how the personification of society was used to lambast free exchange as equivalent, at least in some instances, to naked theft.

The hypostatization of society led not only to the fabrication of a public interest superior to the welfare of the individual but also to the idea that all resources (or a significant portion thereof), whether intellectual or material, were held in common. The myth of community ownership, the possession of all goods by the "people as a whole," was an integral part of the entire collectivist position. Basically, society was portrayed as the author of all benefits and, consequently, the producer of all wealth. Now, if society was the sole real entity, then only it was capable of acting and accumulating capital. Hence, so the reasoning went, all the citizens of the nation, and not just the few, were entitled to an appropriate share of the wealth produced by the community, because all equally were component parts of the whole and all had, in some sense, made a contribution to the well-being of the social organism.

Thus, one finds writer after writer making little or no reference to the factor of personal capacity or to initiative in the creation of wealth, other than intimations that the inequalities found in the free market were exaggerated and not truly reflective of the various individual contributions to the whole. On those infrequent occasions when it was deemed necessary to refute those who brought to the fore the role of individual ability in the creation of material goods, the collectivist theorist trumpeted that the few had plundered the masses of men, that the rich had become rich by exploiting the poor honest laborer.

In contrast to orthodox socialism, no specific theory of value usually was introduced; a simple declamation against the rich was considered sufficient proof of their parasitism. For instance, Lester Ward remonstrated that merchants and bankers had grown wealthy by the "mere handling of the objects" that the mechanic had made. Admitting that some may have more ability than others, he distinguished between the pecuniary trickery of those who flourished on the free market by living off the efforts of others and the mental acuity of those who bettered the condition of mankind, without fundamentally justifying or enlarging upon the distinction. "Some have more (intellectual) power than others," he wrote, "and by means of it they withdraw property from the weaker ones according to the law of acquisition above set forth. . . . But, when they [advocates of "brain-titles"] assert that the brain-power which qualifies a man to accumulate the wealth that others have created is the same brain-power that moves the wheels of social progress, they commit a very serious mistake."[19] Neither Ward nor any of the other theoreticians who sympathized with this sentiment offered a systematically worked-out doctrine of interindividual economic exploitation, discovering instead that it was more profitable to concentrate their attention on society and simply to attest that the capitalist plundered the collective, transferring its wealth to his pockets. This depiction of society as an organic whole, sometimes blended with the idea that wealth was a static quantity, engendered views that some were taking more than, and others therefore getting less of, their proper allocations and that great inequalities in wealth were ipso facto the result of a privileged few enriching themselves at the expense of the community. *no. John Taylor*

Henry George, of course, was the first prominent figure to bring the question of the distribution of wealth before the American public. In his writings, particularly *Progress and Poverty* (1879), there is a continual glorification of equality. The widening of the gap between rich and poor was George's central concern, and it was this situation, and not any notion of rights, which motivated him to investigate the "problem," as he himself testified. Both his posing of the question and his solution were sketched in collectivist terms. Reifying society, he assumed that the great material progress which had been achieved had come about as the result, not so much of individual effort, but of a communal striving; society was the key factor in America's industrial development. Yet, although the community was producing the benefits, it was not acting in its own welfare. It was permitting a few rapacious owners of land to confiscate the "unearned increment" at the expense of the mass of the people, thereby creating an iniquitous gap between the very rich and the very poor. The government, therefore, acting in the name of society, should simply collect all rent and use it so as to profit the community. This visualization of society as a real existent acting in accordance with its own interests and distributing wealth to enhance its welfare was unabashedly collectivist, regardless of whether rent be just or unjust. Furthermore, George's reasoning could just as easily be applied to the whole of economic activity, especially in a highly industrialized society where production is dependent upon a complex network of exchange.[20] Indeed, succeeding writers did not turn away from this implication and, no doubt drawing some of their inspiration from George's approach, propounded that society should be regarded as either the principal or, more often, the exclusive force in the accumulation of capital.

This holistic tendency found general favor in the period and was most noticeable in the writings of Edward Bellamy. Rather surprisingly, Bellamy, whose *Looking Backward* attained substantial circulation, had a great impact on both popular and scholarly thought. Possibly this was due to the fact that in his works he united almost every collectivist argument originated in the nineteenth century into a rough, yet readable, synthesis. In any case, his constant and ubiquitous reification of the community made it possible for him sometimes to ignore and always to downplay the importance of individual achievement in the creation of material values. Everyone, he stipulated, was entitled to an equal portion of the produce of the social organism, for society "collectively can be the only heir to the social inheritance of intellect and discovery, and it is society collectively which furnishes the continuous daily concourse by which alone that inheritance is made effective." Because it is society, and not the individual, which creates a limited wealth, the ideals of equality and justice dictate that no man "appropriate" from the general stock an unfair portion. Thus, it "follows that if some have a disproportionate share, the rest will not have enough and may be left with nothing. . . . The state must evidently see to it that the means of life are not unduly appropriated by particular individuals, but are distributed so as to meet the needs of all." Bellamy's coach parable, which likened society to a hunger-driven coach pulled by the oppressed masses, was another projection of this tissue of assumptions. It conveyed the idea that in a system of free exchange and private ownership, the acquiring of wealth involved no productive ability, intelligence, or dedication but was merely a question of grabbing the seats.[21]

From a similar, if less radical, standpoint, Herbert Croly assaulted the reward of millionaires as exorbitant and called for collective action to remedy the situation. He felt that the point at which the individual was remunerated in excess of his services to society was a difficult one to define, but, and the influence of Henry George is obvious here, he suggested that the community confiscate in taxes at least those increases in wealth due to a general increase in population and business. Henry Lloyd spoke of the gifts of nature that had supposedly been given to mankind in common, such as lands, mines, and industrial sites, and maintained that they had been turned from service to selfishness. Like many of his fellow reformers, he took the creation of wealth and the conversion of raw materials into finished products as occurring practically automatically and as the fulfillment of a social function, devoting little or no attention to the factors of risk and effort. He readily adopted the fiction that wealth was truly and originally owned by all and somehow existed in a state of nature prior to being transformed by human action. Hence, only low chicanery, and not talent, could explain the emergence of great fortunes. They depended on nothing more than sleazy manipulation, the pillaging of the community by a vicious few. "The prize we give the fittest is monopoly of the necessaries of life, and we leave these winners of the powers of life and death to wield them over us by the same self-interest with which they took them from us."[22]

James Allen Smith wrote in the same vein when he referred to individuals in the free market selfishly taking from the assets of society more than they had contributed to it. "Laws, institutions and methods of trade which make it possible for the individual to take from more than he adds to the general resources of society tend inevitably toward general social deterioration." Thorstein Veblen censured the practices of business and avowed that wealth was a communal possession. The incompetent businessman, in his quest for pecuniary gain, had made his fortune by robbing society; "it is felt that he best serves the common good who, other things equal, diverts the larger share of the aggregate wealth to his own possession. His acquiring a defensible title to it makes him the putative producer of it." And Walter Weyl pointed up the exploitation of the community engaged in by the wily trust. Without offering any theory of value, he denounced the trust as parasitically absorbing the resources of society, becoming rich not by the exercise of efficiency but by virtue of a predatory cunning. "The trust," he revealed, "has played on the community's surplus, and the insider has preyed on the trust. From those who work for the trust, seek to compete with the trust, buy from the trust or sell to the trust, a steady stream of wealth flows *to* the trust."[23]

What is most conspicuous about this theory is the virulent animadversion directed at those who had achieved a much greater prosperity than their fellow men. That wealth was "appropriated" or "diverted" from the general stock was not unjust; what was evil was its greatly unequal distribution. Few writers cared to advocate strict economic equality, yet almost all insisted that inequality should be reduced, by whatever means possible. There was, to be sure, understandable evasion about the exact standard by which the social capital was to be allocated. To specify in detail how the individual components of the "social organism" were contributing to the amassing of material goods would be to introduce a dangerously nonsocial factor, one concentrating on what the individual had "earned," and any extensive discussion based on these lines would tend to undermine the conception of society as an entity and wealth as a communal product. It was simply presumed that while "all of us" were collectively bringing into existence the riches of the nation, some of us were taking more than our "rightful share," which was never exactly defined. In logic, there was no reason why one could not conclude that there was not enough inequality, but the sentiment invariably induced by conjuring up the image of a united, toiling humanity was such that the more prosperous segments of the population were singled out as exploitative. The claim of the entrepreneur to superior reward, based on superior ability, was thereby gainsaid.

The premise of ontological collectivism did not serve only to overturn the system of material distribution under a regime of free contract. Present, whether tacitly or explicitly, in almost all the deliberations of reformers, it played a critical role in their demonstration that the state could not be limited by the rights of the individual, abstractly conceived. The hypostatizing of society cleared the way for a general subversion of individualism and its replacement by a statism designed to further the "social interest." What was involved here was a total reversal of the republican faith in the autonomy of politics. The political order was now made dependent on the social. The personification of society and the transmuting of man into a cell, one among many, of the social organism made it possible to envision government, not as a mechanical construction intended to protect rights, but as a servile instrument devised to carry out the will of "society as a whole." It followed that the belief that two spheres of action, the private and the public, could exist side by side harmoniously had to be rejected. The reification of society set the stage for a sweeping transmogrification of the political concepts of republican individualism into social constructs.

CHAPTER IV

THE PRAGMATIC REJECTION OF ABSOLUTES

The years after the Civil War were characterized by conspicuous change in practically every field of human endeavor, from the industrial to the political. It is understandable, then, that a philosophy positing change as the essence of reality would be accorded a favorable reception; and this was, in fact, the case with pragmatism in America. But it is crucial to recognize that pragmatic modes of thinking antedated the formulation and propagation of pragmatism as a relatively systematic and explicit philosophy. It cannot be said that those who emphasized the practical at the expense of the theoretical adhered to all the main positions and tendencies of pragmatism that were to be found in the writings of Charles Peirce, William James, and John Dewey; they were in substantial agreement, however, with many of its key tenets. Reciprocally, the founders of pragmatism refined, elucidated, expatiated upon, and made philosophically respectable existing modes of thinking characterized by a hostility toward abstract theory.

The intellectual rebellion against the limited state was formulated predominantly in pragmatic terms.[1] The critics of free government counterposed facts to theory and experience to dogma, and they insisted that practical consequences, and not the ejaculations of a priori theorizers, should serve as the touchstone by which to judge action. Progressives found facts which, as they construed them, indicated that free exchange, in an increasing number of cases, was producing undesirable consequences. The differences among most of the opponents of the existing order did not revolve so much around fundamental philosophical principles as around questions of the degree to which limited government had failed. Such men as Edward Bellamy and Thorstein Veblen were, for instance, considerably more radical in their suggestions for reform than

The Pragmatic Rejection of Absolutes 71

the great majority of their fellow collectivists, but their thought was just as much oriented to the practical. Bellamy did project a socialist utopia, but he was careful to exclude from it many of the features of orthodox socialism, such as atheism, material- ism, class character, and dogmatism. His criticism of capitalism was made in pragmatic and not theoretical terms.

Pragmatism as an explicitly formulated philosophy did not exert great influence until after the turn of the century; and its effect, given the predilections of the collectivist intellectuals for the "practical," was not innovative. What James and particularly Dewey were able to accomplish was not to stimulate new approaches to human problems, as James admitted when he called pragmatism a new name for old ways of thinking, but to systematize the various pragmatic tendencies into a coherent whole. This achievement enabled the critics of free government to launch a more sustained and conceptually rigorous attack against it, one which, while addressing itself to specific prob- lems in a particular context, would not limit itself to them. In this regard, James Allen Smith's comment on the role of Dewey is especially enlightening. "We were all Deweyites before we read Dewey and we were all the more effective reformers after we had read him."[2] The popularity which pragmatism attained so quickly in America can be explained only by the fact that it elaborated, systematized, and sanctioned, in philosophical ter- minology, modes of thinking which, before its advent, had existed in inchoate form. The reformist movement had been groping about in the dark, searching for an appropriate philosophy which would be congenial both to its aims and methods, and pragmatism, appearing on the scene at the right time, became that philosophy.

It may be asserted that pragmatism was deeply influenced by the theory of evolution, at least as the latter was interpreted by the mainstream of intellectuals. Although the period after the Civil War has been characterized often as one in which a pseudoscientific social Darwinism was made to function as a convenient rationalization for a predatory capitalism, the fact remains that the overwhelming majority of progressives were just as prone as the paladins of free government, and probably more so, to invoke Darwin's theory and to attempt to employ the concepts found in it in the social sciences. As has been shown, most of the scholarly protagonists of free government did not cast their views in a social Darwinistic framework, and in so far as they made use of evolutionary terminology at all, it was in a wholly ancillary manner.

Organic theories of the state had been composed, of course, prior to the publication of *The Origin of Species* in 1859, and such theorists as Brownson and Mulford, writing immediately after the Civil War, borrowed largely from European political thought, notably the German, in demonstrating that the state was an organic structure, not bound by written documents. Still, the specific application of Darwin's evolutionary hypothesis to history and human institutions engendered a revolutionary impact on American political thought in several important ways. First, the belief that evolutionary theory concerned itself with the preservation of the species shifted attention from the individual to the collective. Second, Darwin's rejection of the immutability of biological species led to the notion that change lay at the core of reality. Society was now perceived as a constantly changing living structure, not a fixed entity. Third, the concept of the physical surroundings that determined which "variations" were to survive was transformed into that of a social milieu. Political evolution, it was claimed, had to respond to changes in the social environment. Pragmatism incorporated these intellectual deductions made from Darwinism into an explicit philosophy.[3] Indeed, as Philip Wiener has shown, pragmatism, in almost all its varieties, arose out of the theory of evolution. Its chief exponents, Peirce, James, and Dewey, consciously borrowed from it.[4]

However much it derived inspiration from evolutionism, pragmatism certainly did not confine itself to a mechanical transference of various propositions from the biological realm to the arena of human action. Instead, pragmatism was intent on constructing an entire world view from the belief that change was the essence of reality. The negation of theory, relativism, the seeking of the meaning of concepts in effects, and a host of other conclusions were all distilled from this fundamental insight. But of interest here are two characteristics of pragmatism, its community bias and, particularly, its insistence that truth could not be a static attribute. Both left a substantial and lasting imprint on thinking about politics.

Peirce's theory that truth was simply that which a community of observers would arrive at in the long run collectivized truth.

In addition, Peirce equally made truth a product of consciousness, which was regarded not as the perceiver but as the creator of reality. Truth, then, was both communal and subjective, because it was dependent upon the state of consciousness of a collective, in this case defined as the community of investigators. William James departed from Peirce's position, at least on a superficial level, but he also cleared the way for John Dewey. James typically has been appraised as an individual-oriented theorist, in contrast to Dewey, usually portrayed as essentially community-oriented.[5] The former advocated a radically subjectivist view of truth and generally discussed the individual, whereas the latter returned to Peirce's collective subjectivism, accentuating the social self. James, nevertheless, was by no means hostile to political collectivism,[6] and his concept of experience could easily be extended to encompass common activity, as it was by Dewey. In fact, it was James's undermining of reason that set the stage for Dewey's explicit assault on individualism.

James conceived of truth as a relationship between subject and object, one which involved the former's participation in the construction of reality. Truth was not something to be predicated of an external, objective reality but was made by the completion of the experiential process. "The truth of an idea is not a stagnant property inherent in it. Truth *happens* to an idea. It *becomes* true, is *made* true by events. Its verity is in fact an event, a process: the process namely of its verifying itself, its veri-*fication*. Its validity is the process of its valid-*ation*."[7] James underscored the activity of the agent in initiating events and validating the facts and thereby made truth dependent upon consciousness, at least in part.[8] In contrast to Dewey, he usually concerned himself with problems that confronted the individual, such as the existence of God, and seldom spoke of society as such. But to expound that the process involved was a collective one and that men were so interrelated in their activity that a private, nonsocial individual did not exist was to extend logically James's radical subjectivism. If reality is to be found in the process, then it follows that the very existence of the abstract individual is in doubt. If this were the case, then the notion of an individual consciousness interacting with the environment and thereby churning out truth would be erroneous, for it would fail to take into account the complex relations existing among men. The multiplicity of consciousness would have to be disavowed, and society, not the individual, would emerge as the central fact. This was the line taken by Dewey, who retained James's subjectivism and added a compatible element, the extension of the concept of process to the totality of interactions occurring in the society.[9] Pragmatism, in the hands of Dewey, ended up submerging the individual in the collective, reifying the society and the group and treating the individual as a sum of social connections. One can cite Dewey endlessly to the effect that the individual apart from the collective has no real existence, that his very essence is social, that the public interest, superior to any possible interest of the individual, is the standard by which to gauge action, and that individuality is realized only by engaging in communal activities for "social" purposes. Dewey's deification of the community made truth a result, not of individual caprice as James had asserted, but of the emanations of a collective consciousness.

Pragmatism not only laid stress on the subjective nature of reality. It also held that reality was fluid, constantly in a state of flux, varying both temporally and with regard to certain factors. James protested against the "block universe" and wished to substitute a pluralism for a stultifying monism, and Dewey, with his emphasis on experimentalism, shunned the rigidity of the a priori.[10] Pragmatism, then, disdained the Absolute and affirmed a sweeping relativism. It maintained that truth may vary with different conditions and that it was dependent upon the selected context. The conception that truth was not eternal and universal but was forever changing was incorporated into the collectivist outlook. From it sprang the notion that free government had only limited applicability and that it definitely could not claim timeless validity, as its advocates were wont to assume.

The demise of the belief in natural rights took place in the context of both the repudiation of absolutes and the affirmation of the metaphysical priority of society. For the early American revolutionary theorists, natural rights were absolutely fundamental. They were normative abstractions defining man's freedom of action in a political context; from them alone were to be derived the principles of political obligation. The American idea consequently made the state the fruit of volition and did not represent it as a natural growth superior to human ratiocination. The individual was placed at the center of the system, and it was he who had rights, not society. Such rights were held to be universally and timelessly valid, stemming from the nature of man.

With very few exceptions, reformers after the Civil War spurned the doctrine of natural rights as archaic and not suited to the needs of a changing society. Their attitude was best expressed by Washington Gladden when he remarked that the "entire result of putting the emphasis of our thinking, our teaching, our discussion upon rights is to develop an unsocial temper, a disposition to seek our individual good at the expense of the community."[11] The issue of rights was conceived in terms of the individual versus the community, and just as with the production of wealth, it was believed that by claiming natural rights, the individual was thrusting himself forward "at the expense of the community," morally, intellectually, and, of course, materially. Again, it was never detailed exactly how the individual was exploiting the collective. This fact was rather loosely brought forth from the assumption that society was an entity, possessing all material and spiritual goods and reserving all rights of action to itself.

Some of the early collectivist theorists did descant that man had natural rights, yet they clung to the label while rejecting the substance. Brownson averred their existence, while at the same time observing that it was the nation as organism which gave them meaning and reality. Although Mulford also affirmed them, he declared that they were not absolute or inalienable, noting that there were none which could not be "abridged or yielded or interrupted" and that the rights of the nation were precedent to those of the individual.[12] Henry George did insist that his proposed solution of the "problem" of inequality vindicated natural rights, particularly the right to property, but the whole structure of his thought was drawn in collectivist terms.

Succeeding reformers did not pretend that they were protesting against free government in the name of natural rights. Although they retained the notion of rights, they gave it an entirely new signification. Essentially, adversaries of the limited state started from the premise that society was ontologically prior to the individual, who could not even be thought of apart from the complex of social relationships in which he found himself from birth onwards. For this reason, it is erroneous to speak of the individual as if he were a discrete entity, independent of other men. Society, and not the individual, must be taken as the "given," as the point of reference. Rights, therefore, are not to be ascribed of isolated individuals, nor are they the foundation on which the state is erected. They are a communal product which derives from the fact that men live in society. It is the state, acting as an instrument of society, which confers rights on its citizens and decides what privileges they shall enjoy. To think otherwise is to be guilty of the fallacy of believing that individuals exist antecedent to society. Furthermore, it was noted that the conception of natural rights was a static one, absolute in its character and allowing for no changes in conditions. Because concepts could never be fully representative of a reality in flux, notions formed at an earlier time could easily become obsolete at a later period.

Harry Elmer Barnes, for instance, attested that the consensus of sociological thought in the post–Civil War period postulated rights as the "rules of the game" in the social process, accepted and applied by the community in law. They were not the possession of a hypothetical individual but were actually the product of societal interaction and were necessary for the survival of the "social organism." "No such thing as the abstract isolated individual is known to social science. Nor are individual rights metaphysical entities. They are but concrete lines and types of sanctioned action essential to the orderly and efficient functioning of the social organism as a whole; and as such they are originated, determined, defined and limited by social interests and necessity. The rights of man are in no sense primordial abstractions to which society has to adjust itself and for the protection of which the state was specifically created." Roscoe Pound, who gave the most systematic treatment of the question of rights, observed critically that the juristic theory of natural rights was thoroughly individualistic and, therefore, flawed by false premises. "As a theory of inherent moral qualities of persons it was based on deduction from the nature of the abstract, isolated individual." Lester Ward declared that the "metaphysical conception of abstract right" should be banished and that society could not be bound by the fictions of inalienable rights and the social contract. "The question of right," he wrote, "can be disposed of with a word. We do not care to discuss the question as to whether society or any other organism has a right to manage itself. Throughout nature the rights of individuals to carry out their desires are limited only by their power to do so." Ward, in solid pragmatic fashion, held forth that the conception of the rights of man was so abstract as to be meaningless, for they did not remotely correspond to concrete reality. They divorced theory from practice, for they had never been fully realized. "The so-called 'abstract rights' of mankind must be denied if society is ever to become the arbiter of its own destiny—in theory, that is, for it is impossible that the real enjoyment of liberty should be thereby in the least diminished, while the sum of human happiness must be greatly increased, and this is the only conceivable object of any right. All the prevailing theories of human rights are but ideal conceptions which not only have never yet been realized, but in the nature of things never can be." Theorists of a similar orientation presented basically the same arguments, maintaining that the individual could not be viewed as something separate from society and therefore as enjoying rights outside the scope of its powers. Westel Willoughby, for example, stated that there were no absolute rights independent of the state and outside its control, and he contended that rights were actually created by society. Similarly, Henry Jones Ford declared that they were not innate but derivative, their actual content being determined by the state. Oliver Wendell Holmes exorcised natural rights from the law by claiming that legal duties could not be inferred from moral abstractions, for they were simply "prophecies of what the courts will do in fact."[13]

Clearly, the principal intellectual advocates of the interventionist state regarded natural rights as the fanciful product of the imagination of individualists. Society, freed from moral law, distributed rights as gifts; men in no sense possessed them by nature. The collectivists projected their view of man into that of rights, conceiving of both as social in character, molded by the "will" of the community.

Many stated, as did Ward, that rights, so long as they remained abstract, were of little consequence and served merely to keep the masses obedient. Hence, the state, by intervening in the lives of its citizens, was guaranteeing what had been promised to them, making a reality of the ideal. Even here, however, the rights that were to be secured were not "primordial" but epiphenomenal, since the community considered its interests in deciding which ones were to be permitted to individuals. In any case, progressives denounced the purely formal character of natural law and called upon the state to reconcile theory with practice. This theme is again a common one and can be found in the writings of multifarious theorists, particularly in those of Bellamy, Ward, Weyl, and Dewey.

The line of reasoning embarked upon was that a right should be envisioned as a demand having an unconditional claim to satisfaction, regardless of means. In fact, it was identified with a definite consequence; in accordance with the pragmatist intoxication with process and distaste for absolutes, right was not construed as the power to act, only as a result. In so far as the desired result was not achieved, no right could be said to exist. In pragmatist thinking, capability was an empty concept, devoid of any kind of experiential reference, and the positing of right as the power to accomplish an action was correspondingly regarded as specious. Because processes constituted reality, only activity realizing a goal could be defined as a right. Consequently, natural rights as understood individualistically under free government resulted in their own negation. Only a privileged few actually possessed them and enjoyed what had been promised to all the people. *Ergo,* the rights postulated in the Declaration of Independence could only be made real by summoning forth state power. "The inner soul of our new democracy is not the unalienable rights, negatively and individualistically interpreted, but those same rights, 'life, liberty, and the pursuit of happiness,' extended and given a social interpretation."[14]

Lester Ward's criticism of natural rights as ideals bearing no relation to the reality of the human condition was fully in accordance with this argument. He pronounced that the outcome was of sole importance. To be deprived of rights was the same thing as to be deprived of property, and the lack of property was prima facie evidence that someone's rights had been violated. Edward Bellamy, who advocated a more complete form of collectivism than any other intellectual reformer of stature, asserted that the nationalist revolution would render society the ruler of its own affairs, actually rescuing the right to property, which had been subverted by the capitalists. Personal control, Bellamy claimed, was not perceived as essential to this right even in the heyday of capitalism; the state, by preventing the looting of the community by a minority, would secure it by ensuring that all would have material goods. John Dewey believed that rights could be assured only when society as a whole guaranteed their fulfillment. Otherwise, they would remain abstract, detached from experience. "Until there is secured to and imposed upon members of society the right and the duty of work in socially serviceable occupations, with due returns in social goods, rights to life and free movement will hardly advance much beyond their present largely nominal state."[15]

It was made clear that all rights were social privileges, granted to the citizen in order to promote the general interest. These rights, however, implied social obligations. Consequently, none of the social rights could be enjoyed without incurring some kind of liability. Rights were correlative with duties.

Absolute rights, if we mean by absolute those not relative to any social order and hence exempt from any social restriction, there are none. But rights correspond even more intrinsically to obligations. The right is itself a social outcome: it is the individual's in so far as he is himself a social member not merely physically, but in his habits of thought and feeling. He is under obligation to use his rights in social ways. The more we emphasize the free right of an individual to his property, the more we emphasize what society has done for him. . . . The only fundamental anarchy is that which regards rights as private monopolies, ignoring their social origin and intent.[16]

It was only apparently paradoxical that, as rights were expanded, the number of duties correspondingly increased. Individuals who enjoyed the full gamut of social rights were also those who were most closely bound to the community and subject to its needs. Although the concept of duty was interpreted in an abundance of ways, one of its precepts was invariably that the individual owed his life and all his possessions, both moral and material, to society, which could draw upon them whenever it deemed expedient and use them in the manner best fitting its interests.

The social interest became the common denominator of all the new rights established by the positive state. Walter Weyl wrote that it is "this social interpretation of rights which characterises the democracy coming into being, and makes it different in kind from the so-called individualistic democracy of Jefferson and Jackson." Walter Lippmann in the same spirit took social use as the criterion by which property would be controlled and allocated, declaring that the "community is engaged in a competition with rich men as to which can make the better use of the nation's wealth. There is no question of inalienable rights. It is a question of good use and bad use, wise use and foolish use."[17] Although other writers on politics made similar comments, few discussed in meticulous detail the exact relationship of rights to the social interest. All used the concept in generally the same way, as implying the subordination of men to the collective and as determining rights and duties apart from any consideration of the abstract individual. Roscoe Pound was one of the few theorists of the new social rights who made explicit what had remained implicit in the writings of other collectivists, stating assumptions, clarifying the use of terms, and offering a coherent argument. His views are worthy of attention both because of their representativeness and their explicitness.

Borrowing from Rudolph von Jhering and calling for a pragmatic theory of the law, Pound rejected the existence of the isolated individual, cautioning that while the idea of natural law had its good side (from the pragmatic standpoint), it ultimately had bad effects. It resulted in the conceptions that society and the individual were antithetical, the latter needing to be protected from the former, and that the law was absolute, securing personal rights and therefore unresponsive to human needs.

Perhaps nothing has contributed so much to create and foster hostility to courts and law and constitutions as this conception of the courts as guardians of individual natural rights against the state and against society, of the law as a final and absolute body of doctrine declaring these individual natural rights, and of constitutions as declaratory of common-law principles, which are also natural-law principles, anterior to the state and of superior validity to enactments by the authority of the state, having for their purpose to guarantee and maintain the natural rights of individuals against the government and all its agencies.[18]

Pound adhered to the idea that the whole was more than the sum of its parts and that the individual was a social unit. Thus, the concept of natural rights existing prior to the state or society was nugatory. But he went beyond these declarations, usually regarded as sufficient in themselves to discredit the individualistic position, combining the subjectivism of James with the instrumentalism of Dewey.

Pound held that the change from natural law to the socialization of law began when it was recognized that interests lay behind rights. The state did not create these interests, which may be individual, social, or public, for they arose out of the competition among individuals, groups, and societies. It is the task of the law to determine which interests shall be accorded official recognition, what their limits are, and how conflicts will be settled among them. A radically subjectivist conception of interests is offered, for they may be defined as claims "which a human being or group of human beings may make." Hence, whatever the individual, or the group, happens to value can be presented to the community as a claim. Pound went on to define the social interest as that of the "community at large," though he did not expatiate upon this definition. He merely asserted its existence and conveyed the idea that it was primordial and not derivable from any individual or group interest. Defined in such a way, it was clearly something which could only be predicated of a supraindividual society. As for the law, it existed to serve the social interest and rights were simply what it decreed. Individual claims, of course, were consulted in the process of ascertaining the law, but they did not give it content. The social interest served as the yardstick by which to judge the worth of various claims and to decide which ones would be given legal sanction and which would not. The interests of the individual, therefore, were of significance only in so far as they promoted the social interest, and not because of any intrinsic importance. Such rights as are granted to individuals, then, are only means to implement the interests of society. It follows that the problem of legislation is not to "balance" individual and social interests but to harmonize a given "social interest with other social interests and to weigh how far this or that individual interest is a suitable means of achieving the result which such a balancing demands."[19]

The appraisal of the claims of individuals, Pound thought, must be made within the framework of the social interest. No demand can be granted which would run counter to it. Consequently, if an individual wishes to have the state secure an interest, he must demonstrate that it would accrue to the benefit of the public. No propounding of an innate right to life would suffice. Thus, "while individual interests are one thing and social interests another, the law, which is a social institution, really secures individual interests because of a social interest in so doing. Hence it would seem that no individual may claim to be secured in an interest that conflicts with any social interest unless he can show some countervailing social interest in so securing it—some social interest to outweigh that with which his individual interest conflicts."[20] This new theory of rights, then, emphasized their social nature, holding that they were claims sanctioned by society. A claim was not a call for abstract freedom of action, at least not usually; it was any demand presented by an individual or group, all possessing the privilege of staking a claim to some portion of the community's goods. Human wants, precisely because they were relative and subjective, were metaphysically and morally equivalent. Such being the case, there was no prior reason why the desire of one individual to be left alone in the enjoyment of his life and property should be considered in any way superior to the demand of another that the community confiscate the property, and direct the efforts, of others for his benefit. Rights were only those desires of individuals which were compatible with the interests of society and enacted into law by it. By the grace of the social interest, that which had been relative to the individual and constituted "truth" for him was thaumaturgically transmuted into something objective, binding on all, to be respected by all, and constituting "truth" for all. Subjectivism had been collectivized.

A theme which appeared more and more frequently toward the end of this period was that of human rights versus property rights. Particularly, in campaigning for the presidency, both Woodrow Wilson and Theodore Roosevelt affirmed that a conflict existed between the two and that the government should be the servant of human needs, not the tool of property. Wilson pronounced that "what I am interested in is having the government of the United States more concerned about human rights than about property rights." Roosevelt said that the "man who wrongly holds that every human right is secondary to his profit must now give way to the advocate of human welfare, who rightly maintains that every man holds his property subject to the general right of the community to regulate its use to whatever degree the public welfare may require it."[21] The contention that a conflict obtained between property and human welfare was not something new added to the collectivist position. It was derived from the general theorems previously outlined or, rather, was a restatement of them in another form. By property rights was meant the system of absolute natural rights which existed anterior to the state. They were possessed by "isolated" individuals and served as the foundation on which the state was constructed. By human welfare was meant the notion of right as a social product. The denial of the right to property was the explicit scrapping of the concept that any man was intrinsically entitled to order his actions as he saw fit, so long as he did not employ force or fraud. It was definitely implied that the chief beneficiaries of "human rights" would be the great mass of the people and that such deprivation as would be inflicted would be largely at the expense of the rich. In other words, the implementation of the doctrine that human welfare was superior to property signified in practice that property would be confiscated from some, through legislation, and distributed to others, thereby satisfying a variety of "human needs." This supposed dichotomy was, in fact, merely a reiteration of the socialized theory of rights in a more appealing and convincing form.

The revolutionary import of the social conception of right was that the individual was now subject to the caprice of society and its chosen instruments. Rights had been regarded previously as a limitation on the power of the rulers. They defined the sphere of action in which men were free to operate, and government was only the organ empowered to protect them. Furthermore, they were not, and did not originate in, a claim on the efforts of others. Their reality did not consist of an actual process or a predetermined result, only in the liberty to function. The right to property was not the right to obtain property by whatever means necessary, including force, nor was the right to happiness the right to be happy by enslaving others. In the one case, as in the other, the right inhered in the freedom to pursue a course of action consonant with the like freedom of others, without any guarantee that the goal sought would be actually reached. But the theory that rights were a gift of the community and that they pertained to a concrete result overturned entirely the conception of the Founding Fathers. The allegedly metaphysical law of nature, to whose requirements men were morally bound to conform, was replaced by the supposedly self-evident "will of the whole," whose dictates men had, unquestionably and just as absolutely, to obey. To make rights (or, more precisely, demands) more than empty abstractions required that men be treated as interdependent units, all having a claim on all. The only way to execute such a doctrine was through force wielded by the state in the name of society.

Thus, it came about that rights were transformed from a protector into a destroyer of man's freedom. They became a prescription for the enlargement of the coercive power of the state, not a check upon it. The more the number of rights was expanded, the more the citizen found himself subject to human needs, as interpreted by the spokesmen of the community. Each new right inevitably was held to imply a "social duty" of one sort or another. The change from right as the private possession of the individual to a socially legitimized claim was ingenuously expressed by Roscoe Pound.

Prior to Jhering the theory of law had been individualist. The purpose of law was held to be a harmonizing of individual wills in such a way as to leave to each the greatest possible scope for free action. Such was the view both of philosophical and of historical jurists. Jhering's, on the other hand, is a social theory of law. The eighteenth century conceived of law as something which the individ-ual invoked against society, an idea which is behind our American bills of rights. Jhering taught that it was something created by society through which the individual found a means of securing his interests, so far as society recognized them.'[22]

It may be concluded, then, that the desertion of the political vision of republicanism through the hypostatizing of a dynamic society using government as a tool made it possible to endow the concept of right with a social content.

The undermining of free government was also accomplished through the introduction of a highly relativistic historicism. Both pragmatism and the social interpretation of the evolutionary theory laid great emphasis on the role of change. There was a continual disparagement of the notion of entity and a concomitant exaltation of process and relation, which were usually treated as equivalent to it. Concepts were something static and absolute, separated from experience by an unbridgeable chasm and incapable of ever capturing the essence of the real, held to be in constant flux. They were formalistic and vacuous, concealing rather than revealing the nature of that which existed. Hence, theory was opposed to practice and the ideal to the expedient and convenient.

The notion of absolute truth was discarded, therefore, and a complete relativism affirmed in its place. Because the social environment was in a perpetual state of change and the political was dependent on the societal, no ideal norms of what government should be at all times and in all places could be discovered. In fact, institutions designed to generate certain types of action might eventually produce effects that would be the diametrical opposite of those originally desired. The application of concepts elaborated in a previous period to an environment which had undergone substantial change might conceivably result in their negation in practice. Such was the case with limited government. Changing conditions had rendered it obsolete, and a readjustment of the relationship between the citizen and the state was necessary if the freedom that prevailed at an earlier time was to be preserved. "Legalism" was discarded in favor of the facts.

Perhaps one of the more important expressions of the relativism of this period was the rebellion against the written constitution. Because the nation was a dynamic organism, its development could not be cramped by the formal rules laid out in a document, for this would mean that both the present and the future would be subordinated to the dead past. The behavior of the social organism was not to be regulated by abstract and otiose formulas devoid of any flexibility in their application to concrete life. On the contrary, it was the nation which would give meaning to the constitution, not the constitution to the nation. "The constitution has, in itself, no inherent power and no abstract virtue to deliver the people. It is not for the individual nor for the nation to be saved by any system, however complex, nor any dogma, however subtle. The constitution may become itself only the mask which hides from an age its degeneracy, or the mausoleum which conceals its decay. the pedantry of systems may be made the substitute for living forces."[23] It was reasonable, therefore, that the nation could change the constitution as it saw fit, transforming it so as to accord with the needs of the time. In this way, its substance, if not its form, would be preserved.

Law was, then, not something absolute, to be applied mechanically to the data in question, but fluid and nonobjective. It was to be responsive, not to any abstruse logic, only to the experience of the community. Because this experience was social in nature and society itself was in a constant state of flux, the law could not be fixed. Consequently, it would be impossible to deduce the law from the constitution. Whatever was held to be convenient at any particular time was to determine the substance of the law.

The life of the law has not been logic: it has been experience. The felt necessities of the time, the prevalent moral and political theories, intuitions of public policy, avowed or unconscious, even the prejudices which judges share with their fellow-men, have had a good deal more to do than the syllogism in determining the rules by which men should be governed. The law embodies the story of a nation's development through many centuries, and it cannot be dealt with as if it contained only the axioms and corollaries of a book of mathematics. In order to know what it is, we must know what it has been, and what it tends to become. We must alternately consult history and existing theories of legislation.[24]

The most outstanding feature of this pragmatic relativism was the attack on free government as an outmoded system. In accordance with their collectivist predilections, progressives perceived the advocacy and implementation of the doctrine of natural rights as a metaphysical expression of the needs of American society before the Civil War. At that time, they alleged, the interests of society were advanced by the "let-alone" policy. The American revolutionary theorists had erred, however, in their assumptions that free government was a universally, timelessly valid political system and that individual rights were a bulwark against society, an end in themselves and not a means to the securing of the social interest. In any case, the course followed by the American government before the Civil War conduced, whether intentionally or not, to the public welfare. After the Civil War, the social environment in which the polity functioned had been so greatly transformed that a corresponding transformation of the political system was necessary if a rational adaptation preserving the traditional relationships was to occur. This topic of changing conditions was taken up with a vengeance in the political and sociological literature of this period and occupied an important place in the indictment of limited government. It was an argument particularly attractive to the politicians.

There existed, at least formally, two general positions here. The first held that conditions had changed, so that men should seek to reverse the pernicious developments which had occurred and return to the simplicity of an earlier day. The second admitted that conditions had indeed altered but maintained that the relationships of the past could not be restored and, if restored, could only result in a drastic reduction in the standard of living and a decline in the arts and sciences. Besides, the great industrialization that had taken place had brought men together and made them aware of the pettiness which characterized purely private life, expanding their horizon so as to make them conscious of the common interest. By the end of the period, the latter position had clearly gained dominance, reflected partially in the fact that the advocates of the former tended to reinterpret their views in a way more favorable to consolidation, thereby differing only on the semantic level from those who asserted that big business was here to stay. Nevertheless, even when both camps were at seemingly opposite poles, they shared certain assumptions about the nature of government, freedom, and rights that set them apart from the defenders of free government. Both adhered to relativistic notions of truth and maintained that liberty construed as freedom from the state or society was a specious piece of nonsense, although the proponents of consolidation under the aegis of the national government were clearly more pragmatic in their orientation and also more inclined to take a less rosy view of the Founding Fathers and their work.

It was the societal bias of the critics of free government that made it impossible for them to conceive of a limitation on government as a matter of principle rather than a temporary expedient. Lester Ward acknowledged that what he called laissez-faire had performed a service in the eighteenth century in overthrowing an egoistic class. To this extent, it approximated social action. The advent of the democratic state, however, had made it impossible for an elite detached from the people to seize power and use it for its own benefit. Consequently, social freedom, the last stage of liberty, could now be realized. Westel Willoughby, John Dewey, Theodore Roosevelt, and many others simply restated Ward's argument. Willoughby argued that in the absence of popular government, politics was largely in the domain of individual and class selfishness and that it was therefore natural for the prescription to be against state power. Once the people had become sovereign, this injunction could no longer be true. Dewey wrote that laissez-faire was progressive in its time, for much of government legislation had been despotic. Now, because an irresponsible class had been replaced by the progressive force of democratic government, the common interest could be realized by pursuing a policy of general governmental regulation. In a similar vein, Theodore Roosevelt professed that changing conditions had rendered laissez-faire inapplicable. In so far as government existed exclusively for kings, the history of liberty was written in terms of the limitation of the power of the state. When kings are industrial and financial and the people effectively possess political power, freedom consists in the extension of government functions, not the continuance of the policy of laissez-faire.[25]

Such declarations reveal the lack of any concept of individual right independent of the will of others. What progressives objected to was not the use of force per se but its employment for the benefit of a minority. Essentially, they insisted that freedom from government control was desirable in the past only because any imaginable exercise of force would not have redounded to the "welfare of society as a whole." Were it possible to increase the number of beneficiaries of the policy of force so as to include all the people, and therefore almost all individuals, the situation would be radically modified. This was taken to be the case once the people had obtained control of the governmental machinery. The people, it was assumed, would not act contrary to their own interests. The significance of natural rights, then, was that at the time of their inception, they had performed the function of outlawing not force as such, but of preventing its use by the few at the expense of the many. What was regrettable was that in order to do so, an apparently absolute ban on the power of government to intervene in the life of the nation had to be enacted.

The political aspects of the changes that had transpired, such as the relocating of governmental power in the hands of the people, received less of the reformers' attention than the economic and social features of the new order. In judging the latter features to be more fundamental, progressives denied, once again, the autonomy of politics and reduced it to the servile position of responding to alterations in the socioeconomic environment. Analyzing the structure of society, they averred that great changes in conditions had come to pass and that they had rendered nugatory many of the hallowed aspects of the American political system. This development was held to illustrate the vacuousness of formal concepts, the fact that the usage of the same principle at different times could have entirely different effects. Consequently, new policies, if not new principles, were necessary to retain the substance of the American tradition.

Woodrow Wilson felt that although men had once dealt freely with one another, the growth of business had made relationships impersonal. Depicting Americans as caught up in an economic system which was heartless, he fathomed that the "masters of the government of the United States are the combined capitalists and manufacturers of the United States." With competition increasingly restrained by the capitalists through such devices as the trusts, the small, able competitor was finding it difficult to survive. Social developments exogenous to the political system had led to the new serfdom. "American enterprise is not free, as once it was free. . . . the man with only a little capital is finding it harder to get into the field, and more impossible to compete with the big fellow. Why? Because the laws of this country do not prevent the strong from crushing the weak." Life, complained Wilson, was now more complicated than it had been in the past. New forms of association had arisen that necessitated the expansion of the public sphere, for whenever "bodies of men employ bodies of men, it ceases to be a private relationship." Only by destroying the shackles that the corporations had forged could the citizen and business in general be freed. The only way to accomplish this end was through the exercise of state power.[26]

Henry Demarest Lloyd took a more critical view of the American past than did most reformers. He correctly avowed that the era of free competition and contract was a relatively exceptional one in the history of mankind. Observing with obvious regret the changes that had materialized since the Middle Ages, he expounded that "for three hundred years every one has been scurrying about to get what he could." Nevertheless, despite his dislike for the period marked by the pursuit of gain, he admitted that during this time, society was not highly organized enough to progress except on the basis of private enterprise. Still, he entreated that freedom of trade not be generalized into an inflexible rule. It had only restricted relevance to that era of depravity commencing with the end of the Middle Ages and lasting, apparently, until the latter half of the nineteenth century. Limited government and the maxim of self-interest constituted only a "temporary formula for a passing problem." Society, which had abdicated, was to be enthroned again, and the individual was not to be allowed to follow his caprice in doing what he wished with his own. The changes which had come about had made it possible for the social element to regain its dominant status; "now we are touching elbows again, and the dream of these picnic centuries that the social can be made secondary to the individual is being chased out of our minds by the hard light of the crisis into which we are waking." Lloyd attempted to buttress his position by showing how a given principle, regarded as generating beneficial effects, could entail its own negation when applied to a situation different from the one in which it had originated. Although no friend of competition himself, he noted that extreme competition had actually driven the various competitors out of the field, leaving the monopolist to exploit the people.[27]

This motif of competition destroying competition was an often repeated one and was constantly cited to prove that free trade, while possible in theory, could not obtain in practice; to attempt to implement it would expose the individual to other social powers not specifically governmental in nature. From the pragmatic viewpoint, free production and exchange had become a system discriminating in favor of the rich, although no legislation had been passed to this effect. Again, changes in the social structure had engendered different types of experience and had correspondingly altered the practical import of certain concepts.

Frank J. Goodnow similarly underscored the vacuity of concepts separated from their possible consequences. He cautioned that the character of a government was determined just as much by extralegal as by legal institutions, because both had definite effects on how authority was exercised in the society. He also believed that the rights which the individual was previously thought to possess had to be modified to bring them into accord with the exigencies of modern times. Thus, a dogmatic insistence on minimizing the role of the state as much as possible was unrealistic, given the new conditions that had arisen in the twentieth century. Turning to historical example, Goodnow hypothesized that if it were discovered that federal governments formed in the nineteenth century, such as those of Canada and Germany, had been endowed with greater power than that of the United States, then it would prove that their founders had been guided by facts and not theories. He conjectured that if given a chance to form a new government, the American people would prefer one which would have more authority and which would make the amendment process easier. Finding this to be the case, Goodnow advocated an extension of state power, insisting, in pragmatist fashion, that constitutions should not be regarded as something rigid but as statements of general principle "whose detailed application should take account of changing conditions."[28]

Edward Bellamy and Thorstein Veblen underlined more strongly than most reformers the coercive aspects of industrialization, and they made a more generalized attack on business, not limiting their criticism to trusts or even to big corporations. Bellamy held that in the early phase of American development, industry had not been concentrated and class distinctions had been insignificant. There were many small concerns, none of which had any great capital, and the individual workman was relatively independent of any specific employer, free to change jobs without fear of starvation. But the age of monopoly finally had arrived, rendering the worker powerless against the hugh corporations and exacerbating class conflict. Competition was also snuffed out as the trusts monopolized certain products. The aggregation of capital did make for efficiency, and the restoration of the past system could only be achieved "at the

price of general poverty and the arrest of material progress."
Bellamy, therefore, proposed that political arrangements be
made to conform to social evolution. The economy was to be
nationalized, so that both the substance of freedom, if not its
previous form, and the high standard of living would be
maintained. All capital in his scheme would be controlled by
the state through giant trusts and used for the benefit of the
public.[29]

Veblen, who was influenced by Bellamy, contrasted the
handicraft system to the mode of production prevailing in the
machine age. The instinct of workmanship characterized the
era of handicraft. Industry was conceived of in terms of the
skills and initiative of the individual workman who drew on his
own resources, having been favored neither by ancestry nor by
neighbors. Possessing his own tools, he fashioned things for use
and could produce on his own. The machine process and the
rise of large-scale business changed all of this, rendering the
idea of natural rights inappropriate. Although Adam Smith's
notion of industry was that of manual workmanship, his
practical prescriptions had been extended unjustly to the
industrial age. The natural right to property was a construct
which originated in the period of handicraft. It was also one
"less fully in consonance with the facts of life in any other
situation than that of handicraft." A change in conditions,
namely, the introduction of machines (which were never given
legal status but existed de facto), produced an indirect form of
coercion, making the worker dependent upon the capital of
others. Veblen located the gap between theory and practice
rather earlier than most reformers, affirming that the facts
belied the doctrine of natural rights soon after its propagation.
"Now, through gradual change of the economic situation, this
conventional principle of unmitigated and inalienable freedom
of contract began to grow obsolete from about the time when it
was fairly installed; obsolescent, of course, not in point of law,
but in point of fact." Common sense indicated that the natural
rights conception was no longer adequate and that it should be
replaced by an opposed view.[30]

Some progressives reiterated the topic of changing conditions with little variation. Walter Lippmann simply warned that
the Constitution expressed a policy about certain conditions at
the time it was framed and that problems had subsequently

cropped up which the Founders did not foresee. Charles Van Hise, president of the University of Wisconsin and author of *Concentration and Control* (1912), a work frequently cited by Theodore Roosevelt and his followers in the 1912 campaign, pronounced that the right of price regulation by the state was beyond question and that it had been suspended for a time because it was inexpedient to exercise it.[31] Other critics of free government, all of a strong pragmatist bent, added something to the argument when, delving into the past, they found the Constitution not to be as unsullied as had been thought. They did not scorn the relativistic position that altered conditions required new policies nor did they discover the point of demarcation announcing the reign of exploitation at an earlier date than others. What distinguished their views was both the branding of the Constitution as an antidemocratic document and the acceptance of the economic relationships which existed prior to the Civil War. To be sure, just as with Lloyd, there are elements of wistfulness in their rather reluctant recognition of the free conditions of an earlier day, a manifest, if unacknowledged, desire that men should have been more impelled by "social" motives, and more than a modicum of evident satisfaction over the fact that the self-seeking of all ultimately led to some profiting at the expense of others.

Charles Beard, of course, made famous the thesis that the motives of the Founding Fathers were not abstract justice or the general welfare but the economic benefits which they thought would accrue to them with the adoption of the Constitution. Many of the essentials of his hypothesis had been formulated years earlier in James Allen Smith's *The Spirit of American Government* (1907). Smith held that in the eighteenth century, the conception of government was properly negative, for the conditions of the time dictated that liberty was a limitation on the government's authority. The state was controlled by a minority and could only be used, if used at all, to benefit that minority's interests. The American Revolution, however, wrought a decisive change, for it made the people sovereign. Consequently, there was no longer any need to circumscribe the power of government, which could and should be made a servant of society. The Constitution, in contrast to the Declaration of Independence, was a reactionary document, undemocratic and a product of the political philosophy of the eighteenth century. It was principally economic in character, designed to protect private property and ensure the rule of a few.[32]

Nevertheless, the economic situation mitigated, to some extent, the political injustices perpetrated by the makers of the Constitution. At the time of the Revolution and apparently for some unspecified length of time thereafter, a capital-owning class did not exist, the tools of production were simple and inexpensive, business was on a small scale, and every worker had the opportunity to become an independent producer. Free government was, therefore, not contrary to the interests of the people. The capitalist's lust for profits changed all this, supplanting the democratic system of production with an industrial oligarchy. The factory system forced independent producers down into the ranks of wage earners and made it possible for a cunning, irresponsible few to appropriate the capital of society. This concentration of capital made conditions grossly unequal and worked to the benefit of the new oligarchy and to the detriment of the masses. Free government had the ultimate effect of promoting the interests of a minority clique, thereby altering in its practical meaning. It now expressed nothing more than the selfish viewpoint of a small capitalist class.[33] State intervention was imperative if freedom was to be restored, and such intervention could take place only if political democracy were installed.

Walter Weyl claimed that the democracy of 1776 was a "shadow-democracy," perpetuating slavery and protecting property rights. The Constitution was not written with the needs of "high-priced trust attorneys" in mind, yet it was "especially designed for a class which bore a similar relation to the America of 1787 that the plutocracy bears to the America of 1911." It was undemocratic and served to frustrate the popular will. Weyl highlighted the fact that the much revered pioneer individualism of the early American was, like the Constitution, by no means untainted. "The crass, unbounded individualism of the practical American found its highest expression in private business and the quest for money," and it was this voracity for profit which led to a "brutally unprincipled code of business morals." But in the long run, it was the most intense cultivation of the virtues of self-reliance that resulted in the defeat of individualism. Monopoly was a logical fruit of the selfishness that characterized the behavior of Americans. "The close of the merely expansive period of America showed that an individualistic democracy must end in its own negation, the subjection of the individual to an economically privileged class of rich men."[34] Like Smith, therefore, Weyl perceived the political system established by the Constitution to be reactionary from its inception, whereas the economic system was more congenial to the requirements of the people, due to the wide dispersal of capital, the lack of a gap between rich and poor, etc. Again, like Smith, he saw free government as ultimately conducing to the benefit of a small privileged class, although the legal structure had not been formally altered. To a much greater extent than Smith, he harped on the moral corruption that was inherent in the American tradition right from the beginning, showing how not only free government but also unregulated and sordid self-interest defeated themselves in the end.

Herbert Croly occupied an interesting place apart. He composed his analysis in the form of the conflict between Jefferson and Hamilton. Although he believed that both had faults and that both had virtues, he clearly though Hamilton the greater figure, more percipient and more realistic than his opponent. Croly interpreted Jefferson as pursuing an equalitarian and socialistic result by individualistic means and as being willing to sacrifice liberty to equality. Jeffersonianism was essentially a policy of drift. Hamilton's program, on the other hand, was one of "energetic and intelligent assertion of the national good" and called for the interference of the state to this end. Croly regretted the defeat of Hamilton and the consequent surrender of the American commonwealth to selfishness; still, he reluctantly admitted that when life was relatively simple, the deleterious effects of individualism were greatly circumscribed. "Individual and social interest did substantially coincide as long as so many opportunities were open to the poor and untrained man, and as long as the public interest demanded first of all the utmost celerity of economic development." The Jeffersonian policy, however, was never ideal and finally culminated in its own negation. Economic and social progress changed circumstances drastically and made equality before the law a myth. Free government was no longer nondiscriminatory, at least in practice. It had been transformed into a system benefiting a "few irresponsible men" who had concentrated the financial power of the nation in their own hands. "The economic development of the country resulted inevitably in a condition which demanded on the part of the successful competitor either increasing capital, improved training, or a larger amount of ability and energy. With the advent of comparative economic and social maturity, the exercise of certain legal rights became substantially equivalent to the exercise of a privilege; and if equality of opportunity was to be maintained, it could not be done by virtue of non-interference. The demands of the 'Higher Law' began to diverge from the results of the actual legal system." Free government, reflected in constitutional limitations on the exercise of governmental power, suspicion of the state, and the citizen's responsibility for his own welfare, had to be abandoned if the public interest was to have priority over special interests. A democratic Hamiltonianism had to be fashioned, one which would achieve some of the Jeffersonian ideals by using the power of the state.[35]

In sum, the rejection of free government stemmed quite logically from the pragmatic tendency to set up as the focus of study a changing, hypostatized society. Absolutes proved incapable of surviving in the pluralistic universe. The individual was dissolved in collective processes over which he, qua individual, had little control. Reformers made truth a special prerogative of the community and regarded rights as both claims on the labor of others filtered by the social interest and as patterns of action required for the smooth functioning of the "organic whole." The upshot of this entire development was that they now perceived politics to respond to changes in a highly unstable and complex social environment and thereby dismissed limited government as, at best, a temporary expedient. Still, proponents of collectivism faced the task of substituting something in its place, along with a supporting rationale. The very criticism of republican individualism served not only a destructive function but a constructive one as well, for it contained the analytical framework necessary for the establishment of the "positive" state. Consequently, the conceptual formulation of the new order was made in the same language used to attack the old one.

CHAPTER V

INDUSTRIAL DEMOCRACY AND THE NEW INDIVIDUALISM

In advocating that the "will of the people" be extended to encompass the social sphere, that the state now control, and in some cases prescribe, relationships hitherto considered as purely private, critics of constitutional government did not argue that they were engaging in radical innovation. On the contrary, they insisted that values threatened by social and industrial change would thereby be secured. There was often a difference of opinion as to how the substance of the past was to be preserved. Reformers, however, were in agreement that a true respect for American tradition required "affirmative" action by the state. It was in this context that practically all critics of free government, after having declaimed against the self-seeking and egoism inherent in a market economy, went on to say that collectivism, in all its varied aspects, would actually vindicate a higher form of individualism, providing new avenues for individual growth. They asserted again and again that changes in the structure of society had rendered traditional notions of personal autonomy and self-responsibility obsolete and that the people as a whole had to take cognizance of this fact by extending the powers of the state. Most of the scholars of this period have accepted this view, finding that "the philosophy of the progressive era was therefore individualism, a new individualism designed to give the individual under new conditions, the same kind of advantages enjoyed in a simpler day. It wished to place controls on certain practises of business, not to restrain freedom but to conserve freedom for a greater number."[1]

The adversaries of free government maintained that the old policy of limiting the scope of the state was no longer relevant to modern exigencies and that any attempt to resist the growing power of society could only result in a diminution of individuality. Concepts of individual responsibility, inherited from a preindustrial age, clashed with the concrete situations in which men found themselves, so that stated purpose did not correspond to the actual results ensuing from the implementation of such concepts. Paradoxically, as Roscoe Pound noted, "academic individualism defeats itself."[2]

If "true" individualism could not be realized by following the course of limiting the authority of the state, then only one alternative remained: the increase of society's power over the citizen, through the state if necessary, with the express purpose of bringing men together in a variety of communal activities. The false individualism of the marketplace would be replaced by the higher one based on fraternity. Individualism, in other words, referred not to a state of affairs in which the individual was permitted to seek his interests and live his life free from the interference of the community but rather to an association joining men in a higher unity. "Man isolated and alone develops no individuality of value," wrote Richard T. Ely, "but such individuality is developed only when he lives with and through his fellows. Giving up one's individualism means a growth in individuality." For Henry Demarest Lloyd, as one student of his thought has observed, men "only developed a true individualism when they met in friendly association with their brothers on terms of equality."[3] Other reformers expressed similar sentiments, suggesting that man was not an isolated monad and should not act as if he were.

Lester Ward and John Dewey generalized these ideas into an explicit theory, showing how the increase of political power would result in the association desired, as long as it was wielded by the right people and for the right, that is, social reasons. Ward had been among the earliest theorists who divined that the essence of individualism could be preserved only if its prevailing form were to be subverted. He called attention to the great consolidation that was taking place, considering self-evident its tendency to diminish freedom in so far as it was exempt from social control. Only by rendering unto society that which belonged to society, and that included everything, could the proper circumstances for individual growth be created. "Every step in the direction of true collectivism has been and must be a step in the direction of true individualism."[4] The more society regulated its affairs, the more individualism flourished.

John Dewey sketched the framework in which he chose to

contemplate the question of individualism more than two decades before he published *Individualism, Old and New* (1930), which was merely an elaboration on some of the ideas he vocalized in his *Ethics* (1908), written in collaboration with James Tufts. For Dewey, the central problem was to retain the old individualism, which was a vital part of the American tradition. Judging truth by its consequences, he came to the conclusion that only the devising of new civic agencies could safeguard the old individualism. The main issue, as Dewey saw it, was whether a generalized individualism would triumph over that policy of letting some profit at the expense of others, which he designated as partial individualism. The latter was a product of abstract conceptions divorced from the concrete circumstances that had given birth to them. Applied to America at the turn of the century, they would result in providing freedom of action only for some, presumably the more aggressive and egoistic, but not for all. Those who achieved individuality would have done so by depriving others of a similar opportunity to express their personality.

We may also note that the theoretical principle at issue, the extension versus the restriction of governmental agencies, so far as it is not simply a question of what is expedient under the given circumstances, is essentially a question of a *generalized* versus a *partial* individualism. The democratic movement of emancipation of personal capacities, of securing to each individual an *effective* right to count in the order and movement of society as a whole (that is, in the common good), has gone far enough to secure to many, more favored than others, peculiar powers and possessions . . . the question really involved is not one of magnifying the powers of the state against individuals, but is one of making individual liberty a more extensive and equitable matter.[5]

In sum, the new individualism played up the cooperative links among men and called for an overall increase in the power of the state for the attainment of social ends. Individuality consisted in the participation of the individual in socially valuable activities, not in a hypothetical freedom from society or in the cultivation of such anarchic traits as self-reliance and independent thinking. Political collectivism was the fundamental means by which human capacities were to be set free and association was to be fostered, although other means were certainly not to be discarded. Thus, as a means, it could not contradict the end sought. It was no paradox to avow that the growth of the state was favorable to the emergence of a widely diffused individualism.

To justify their viewpoint, reformers also raised the banner of democracy. They correctly contended that it had been one of the prime ingredients of the "old" individualism. They stressed that the "new" individualism would be equally, indeed more, democratic. Yet, while the label itself was retained, the essence was drastically altered. For republicans, democracy had been first and foremost a political concept, referring solely to the right of the people to select their representatives. It was not conceived as unlimited in scope. Collectivists, on the other hand, drained it of its political content and gave it a social meaning. This development manifested itself in three important ways. First, progressives perceived voluntary relationships as characterized often by the subjection of one individual or group to another, analogous to that involved in governmental control without consent. Second, they held that democracy could legitimately function so as to give direct expression to social "forces," most commonly through removing the safeguards and limitations on majority rule. Third, they saw democracy as residing concretely in the extension of the rule of the people to industrial affairs, particularly over what was termed "monopoly." The market was now in dire need of "democratization."

The major example of subjection was the rise of great corporations not responsible to the needs of the community, a clear threat to rule by the people. Legal relationships had not changed and the people still apparently retained the power to choose their rulers, but under the facade of popular sovereignty existed the effective right of a few to control the destiny of the many, to dispose of their effort in any way deemed suitable. Because the masses of the people were increasingly dependent on the will of a small minority of capitalists for their very subsistence, they could hardly be said to enjoy real freedom or to manage their own affairs. On the contrary, their will was being frustrated constantly by an oligarchy which possessed great wealth and used it to its advantage, setting in a dictatorial fashion the terms of the industrial contract and allowing no voice to the workers. This coercion of capital, forcing the employee to accept the conditions of the employer or seek work elsewhere, was a patent violation of democracy. The economic relationships that men entered into were so crucially a part of their existence that to deny the power to regulate them was tantamount to declaring that they had no right of self-rule at all; oligarchy would be sanctioned in fact, if not in intention.

Basically, progressives took it for granted that individuals had wants and that such wants, under the division of labor, produced social activity designed to satisfy them. Because all were participants in the industrial processes of modern society, all had a right to determine collectively what form social activity was to take and under what circumstances it was to proceed. Production was not something resulting from the employment of individual effort to the creation of material values; it was only the fulfillment of a function crucial to the survival of the social organism. Paradoxically, although the community was responsible for the progress that had occurred, it was not responsible for the fact that some men had arrogated to themselves both the benefits of industrial development and the direction of it. They had not been chosen by society, but they had appropriated, through the use of predatory cunning, the right to control the resources of the nation and to regulate the pace and nature of their exploitation. To have this task of social construction monopolized by a clique would be to violate the canons of democratic equality and to disfranchise the masses by denying them tangible control over their destiny. Some critics, such as Woodrow Wilson, ascertained this to be the case especially with monopoly. "All combination which necessarily creates monopoly, which necessarily puts and keeps indispensable means of industrial or social development in the hands of a few, and those few, not the few selected by society itself but the few selected by arbitrary fortune, must be under either the direct or the indirect control of society."[6]

Others pointed up the general undemocratic tendency of all industry and commerce unregulated by the community, declaring that the power of satisfying human needs was not the exclusive preserve of a minority. Walter Weyl accused those who called for freedom of enterprise of advocating the subjection of the citizens to an autocratic rule. Such freedom was merely a euphemism for tyranny exercised by the few, a situation embodying control without consent for "what this engaging phrase really means is that society, politically organized (and to-day it is only politically that the whole of society is democratically organized), should have no control over the industrial processes by which it lives. Industrial autonomy contemplates a state within a state; an industrial power dividing actual sovereignty with a political power. Industrial autonomy would subject society to business." Brooks Adams similarly assailed owners of capital and industry for wielding an authority which was not theirs by right. "This formidable [economic] power has been usurped by private persons," he thundered, "who have used it purely selfishly, as no legitimate sovereign could have used it." Walter Lippmann referred to J. P. Morgan's "control" of credit as a "colossal autocracy," professing that employers were not "wise enough to govern their men with unlimited power, and not generous enough to be trusted with autocracy. That is the plain fact of the situation: the essential reason why private industry has got to prepare itself for democratic control." Once private enterprise had been subordinated to the will of the people, the remaining problem of collectivism would be to combine popular with administrative power.[7]

It was Edward Bellamy and Henry Lloyd who made the most extended attacks on economic autocracy and who were most vociferous in their support for industrial democracy. Both discerned in unregulated production and exchange oligarchical rule. Bellamy alluded constantly to what he called "economic government," protesting that social evolution had brought about the existence of a new privileged class of rulers. He maintained that "no business is so essentially the public business as the industry and commerce on which the people's livelihood depends," and that consequently, "to entrust it to private persons to be managed for private profit" would be as foolish as permitting government to be run by a nobility. In fact, in a certain sense, monarchy was even better than a "negative" democracy, because the king, for selfish reasons, was concerned with the welfare of the whole, whereas in the latter, the country was despoiled by a few. Lloyd claimed that ideally men did not cooperate in trade for any other purpose than to "mobilize the labor of all for the benefit of all." Yet, in America, there had arisen a class of monopolists who were exercising control without consent. Slavery, of course, had been eradicated, but only because it was the "cruder form of business." A more subtle form of enslavement had come about now, for production was being directed by the desire of a small number for profit. Because the interests of all, including those of an economic nature, constitute the rule of all, democratic principles are fully applicable to the social sphere. "The ability to carry on the business of supplying the various wants of mankind is not a sort of divine right vouchsafed from on high to a few specially inspired and gifted priests of commerce . . . but, like the ability to govern and be governed, is one of the faculties common to mankind, capable of being administered of, by, and for the people."[8]

The main thrust of the criticism directed at "negative" democracy focused upon autocratic rule alledgedly extant in private industry, not upon any corrupt alliance between politics and business. To be sure, progressives stressed that businessmen bought legislatures and generally made politicians subservient to their wills in order to further their own narrow interests; such was the content of much of the muckraking literature of this period. Nevertheless, they always proclaimed that the principal defect of a purely formalistic democracy was that it made possible the usurpation of power by an oligarchy in the era of trusts and combinations, a usurpation which had eventuated without any noticeable change in the legal apparatus. Prominent in this line of thought is the role of the metaphysical premise previously examined, the belief that the whole was more than the sum of its parts. On the basis of this assumption, it naturally follows that no individual or group of individuals may make decisions that will affect others without consulting the will of all.

Discovering despotism in industry, reformers argued that democracy should not be defined exclusively in political terms. Popular rule, they believed, had to make itself felt in social matters as well. Before this situation could exist, the archaic and tiresome restrictions that had been placed upon the operation of government had to be eliminated. In this regard, we see an attempt to overthrow the whole of the Madisonian structure and to produce a basis for government other than individual consent, narrowly interpreted. The barriers to undiluted majority rule were to be torn down. The power of society in all its grandeur was finally to be set free.

Thus, the existing governmental structure was assailed again and again as "undemocratic." Frank Goodnow avowed that no checks on state power should obtain and that government had, therefore, only two functions, politics and administration, the formulation of the sovereign will and its execution. The judiciary was not to pass on the abstract constitutionality of laws, for it was merely a part of the executive. In like fashion, Walter Weyl repudiated the notion of checks and balances and of a division of power as frustrating the will of the people. And Woodrow Wilson admonished that cooperation between branches of government, not warfare, was needed.[9].

More seriously, the Constitution as the supreme law of the land was frequently lambasted. Many reformers sympathized with James Allen Smith's reproach that it was a reactionary and undemocratic document, a creation of eighteenth-century political philosophy. There was also a certain measure of support for making the judiciary at all levels purely elective, with the expectation that it would thereby function as a representative of momentary popular will. Generally speaking, nonetheless, the feeling was that the Constitution should be either "broadly" interpreted or easily alterable, or both. In this way, it would cease to operate as a limitation on the will of the collective. Lester Ward, for instance, disparaged the notion of consent embodied in a constitution as the ground for government. "It is no longer the consent but the positively known will of the governed from which government now derives its power." Herbert Croly, contending that democracy was "impoverished" and "sterile" when "divorced from a social program," advocated that the amendment process be made much more simple. The Constitution, he thought, should be "alterable at the demand and according to the dictates of a preponderant prevailing public opinion." In his view, a simple majority of the electorate should have the right to change it. Justice Holmes, appointed by Theodore Roosevelt to the Supreme Court, objected to a strict, legalistic vision of the Constitution. The majority enjoyed the right to embody its opinions in law, even if the right to contract was infringed. Hence, the Constitution should be interpreted elastically to allow for the current expression of public sentiment. Similarly, Woodrow Wilson reproved those who would endeavor to confine society within narrow limits by a rigid adherence to constitutional norms. All that progressives wanted, Wilson revealed, was to interpret the work of the Founding Fathers according to the Darwinian principle. Finally, James Allen Smith, after stating that the Constitution was designed to thwart democratic rule through the creation of an independent, nonelective judiciary, a cumbersome amendment procedure, and a checks and balances apparatus, called for a return to the spirit of the Declaration of Independence. True liberty, he related, could be achieved only by making of government "an instrument for the unhampered expression and prompt enforcement of public opinion."[10]

The image of society as a whole working its will through political organs made it possible for progressives to demand that government respond directly and immediately to popular desire. Because society could not act contrary to its own, unitary interest, all limitations on majority rule had to be eradicated. The Constitution should be made subject to easy amendment, or it should be construed fluidly, in conformity to "prevailing opinion," and not according to a strict assessment of the words and phrases it contained. For the same reasons, devices that hindered the formulation of the social will, such as checks and balances, were to be rejected. Madison's intricate calculations as to how majoritarian tyranny was to be avoided through the structuring of government were disregarded. There was simply no need to establish filters by which the will of the majority would be purified of tyrannical tendencies. Hence, political theory could no longer be concerned with a "legalistic" study of the state or its offices. As Woodrow Wilson explained, the life of the nation "does not centre now upon questions of government structure or of the distribution of government powers. It centres upon questions of the very structure and operation of society itself, of which government is only the instrument."[11] Again, the social had displaced the political.

Democracy was not only identified with the enthronement of unlimited majority rule and the concomitant devaluing of the concept of the Constitution as a brake on legislative power. In line with the pragmatic predilections of reformers, it was also understood as an actual result, a process bringing about certain consequences. The common inference was that the people, once given power, would act so as to benefit the public interest. Democracy, then, was something more than legalistic machinery, for "in final analysis, however it may be clothed in legal rights and political immunities, democracy means material goods and the moral goods based thereon."[12] The resources of society, both material and ideal, had to be controlled by society itself. Any kind of productive activity lay within the province of the social power, because, in fact, society had given birth to it. Politics and economics, therefore, should be united, and the principle of collective control extended to the industrial sphere. If democracy was so intrinsically good, it did not make sense to limit it to the formal operation of the government. The people had acted collectively in their political capacity, and this had proved that society was not a simple aggregate but a living organism capable of managing its own affairs. What remained was to make industrial life democratic by giving society as a whole the final say on the production and distribution of property.

Hence, reformers portrayed the extension of public control, in one form or another, as making democracy real, as being akin to the assumption of political power by the people. A great number of them thought that the intervention of the state in the economy was a fulfillment of the democratic vision, and they often justified it in these terms.[13] Edward Bellamy, for example, sanctioned the complete nationalization of industry in his utopia by putting forth the claim that it was exactly analogous to making the people the source of political power. "In a word, the people of the United States concluded to assume the conduct of their own business, just as one hundred odd years before they had assumed the conduct of their own government, organizing now for industrial purposes on precisely the same grounds that they had then organized for political purposes." Other reformers simply agreed with Walter Weyl that the coming democracy would be real, not formal, and that it would fix on social ends, carrying over from the political to the industrial field.[14]

The concept of industrial democracy naturally entailed a definite view of competition, its origin, character, and rationale. Now, two broad theories of the economic problems confronting America evolved. Generally, one camp wished to limit the extent of the industrial concentration taking place, so that a state of affairs approximating that of pre–Civil War days could be brought about. The other did not object to industrial size per se, only to abuses that might accompany it. The former evinced a fear of concentrations of power; the latter, a belief that consolidation could be made the servant of public needs. Nevertheless, what differences did obtain between the two were greatly exaggerated, particularly by both parties to the dispute. Those who expressed apprehension at the growth of "industrial power" were equally as willing as those who favored the trend toward consolidation to assert that society as a whole was the master of the government, or ought to be, and that private initiative was a means to the attainment of public goals. They were just as imbued with the collectivist ethos, thinking in terms of a community metaphysically, morally, and politically superior to the individuals who composed it. To be sure, some of the early antitrust legislation, especially in the states, may have been motivated by the belief that it enlarged an abstract freedom of action and that it was required as a condition for any kind of individual growth. But the intellectuals who supported such legislation, however much they may have spoken of a new vindication of the right to property or of the expansion of opportunity, legitimized it by reference to the needs of society, an organic whole. Such benefits as were thought to accrue to the citizens were derivative, resulting from the better performance of a function within the social organism. Society, and not the individual, was the cynosure about which all utilitarian calculations revolved.

In truth, the policy prescriptions of both the friends and foes of the trusts, after the latter had abandoned their all-out opposition to consolidation, were essentially the same. The New Freedom was supposedly an alternative to the New Nationalism.[15] In actuality, the differences between Roosevelt and Wilson were miniscule. Indeed, Herbert Croly, who had helped to inspire the New Nationalism, finally supported Wilson after he acceded to the presidency, and Wilson himself conceded in 1916 that he had practically carried out the program of the Progressive party.[16]

The fundamental assumption permeating all viewpoints was that the industrial system under free exchange and production was autocratic. The problem was to democratize production and make the marketplace responsive to the will of the people, thereby enabling them to exercise greater control over their lives by extending to industry the rights and privileges they enjoyed with regard to the political system. Still, it was in the inherent logic of the arguments employed, whether intended or not, that the concept of monopoly, however restricted its putative area of application may have been, ultimately referred to the individual's right to order his actions in accordance, not with the will of all, but with his own values. Although big business was perceived as more flagrantly undemocratic than small business, it was usually admitted that all property was within the actual or potential control of society. The smaller economic transactions, and some of the larger ones, were not to be interfered with because, in so far as could be divined, they were not harmful to the functioning of the social mechanism.

Henry George was the first major figure to raise the problem of monopoly. Attacking private ownership of the land because it produced an "unearned increment," he proposed that all rent be confiscated in the name of the community. But he believed that monopoly was inherent in other areas of business as well and that the functions of the state could not be reduced to a bald collecting of rent. He did maintain that government could not undertake a general direction of capital and labor. Nevertheless, he strongly felt that because monopoly violated natural rights and the state was the social organ by which all could act, all business that involved monopoly was properly subject to regulation and complete monopolies should be owned by the state. Among the latter were the telegraph, the railroads, the telephone, gas, water, heat, and electricity.[17] Like most reformers, however, he offered no clear idea of monopoly, merely upbraiding it as contrary to democracy, equality, and free trade.

Although other critics of free exchange enlarged upon George's proposals, constantly narrowing the sphere of "free competition," few went so far as Edward Bellamy in his concrete prescriptions. The structure of his thought was fundamentally similar to that of those who looked upon the regulation of the trusts as a way of serving the people. Equally as pragmatic in his orientation, he was less confident of the efficacy of public supervision of industry. Outright state ownership of all the means of production, instead, would do away with most of the disadvantages of private enterprise. The waste from competition, the idling of labor and capital, the limiting of supply to raise prices, the distress produced by periodic crises, and the waste from gluts would be eliminated. Society as a whole would have become the single capitalist, the final monopoly, although one whose profits would be shared by all. Bellamy informed his readers that this result would be a valid expression of the principles of the Declaration of Independence.[18]

Other theorists, sharing Bellamy's bias, ventilated their hostility toward both competition and unregulated combination. The former was a reflection of egoistic individualism. It gave an unfair advantage to the strong over the weak, inculcated habits of mind unfavorable to the ripening of sentiments of community, and culminated in the dead end of monopoly. The latter, so long as it was not socialized, enabled the unscrupulous few who had triumphed in the dog-eat-dog competition to impose their capricious will on the public, to charge what prices they wished for the products that society created and the people needed, and to feel free from the challenge of any kind of countervailing power. Both unrestrained competition and private monopoly were, therefore, subversive of democracy, flouting the will of small competitors and the public at large.

This motif appeared in the writings of both those who eyed the trusts suspiciously and those who greeted them as necessary, efficient tools in the coming collectivization. The former allowed that unlimited competition had led to monopoly and that legislation to curb the excesses of the strong and the crafty was necessary in order to restore free competition. The latter insisted that competition was inefficient and that unregulated monopoly diverted social gains into the pockets of a rapacious minority.

Lester Ward, for instance, expounded that free competition in society was hardly possible and that what competition did exist led to amalgamation. The end result of capitalism was the trust, which suppressed all attempts to dislodge it from its privileged position. Furthermore, Ward declared, competition itself under various circumstances could lead to higher prices. Henry Demarest Lloyd was more specific than Ward in detailing the injustices of capitalism, although he added nothing substantial from the theoretical viewpoint. Competition, Lloyd unremittingly lamented, occurred at the expense of the community and sprang from selfish greed. Those who were intent on profit gave little thought to their fellow men or to their needs. In addition, competition generated consolidation, which was even more injurious to society. Lloyd fulminated against the horrendous practices that he found to exist under free government, a regime both of hectic competition and repressive monopoly. Rebates, cutting prices when rivals entered the field and then jacking them up again after they had been driven out of business, price discrimination, inducing railroads to close their roads to competitors, selling at a loss in certain localities and making up for it by charging higher prices elsewhere were all condemned as vicious acts, as violating democratic equality, as ways of channeling the social surplus into the possession of a few. Lloyd, besides offering little in the way of proof for his allegations, formulated no explicit theory of value, never establishing why a price ought to be at one level rather than another or why one price was arbitrary and another was not. His hatred of inequality and his hypostatizing of society led him to regard private initiative as inherently unsatisfactory. Even when he granted that the trusts had lowered prices, he remonstrated that they had not been reduced enough and that corporation typically set "arbitrary" prices for necessities. As he expressed it in his posthumously published *Lords of Industry* (1910), the "mother-wit of the people knows that prices are not cheap which produce ten-ply millionaires." Lloyd called for a democracy which would have neither rich nor poor and which would regulate business by a variety of means, including public ownership.[19]

Similarly, if in a more moderate tone, such critics of free exchange as Henry C. Adams ventured that competition is "neither malevolent nor beneficent, but will work malevolence or beneficence according to the conditions under which it is permitted to act." The free play of individual endeavor in many instances forced competition down to the lowest level. The state, by altering the plane on which competition worked, could change the effects it produced. Moreover, monopoly was not to be indiscriminately assailed, for it was efficient, although it should be controlled by the state. Both governmental and private activity in the economic realm should exist; there was no need to adopt the outlook of free industry or that of socialism, for the concept of the effects of competition varying with the conditions under which it operated obviated the necessity to choose either extreme.[20]

Almost all progressives envisaged competition as referring to a specific pattern of behavior, one which conformed to preconceived standards. Whether it was imagined as good or bad or dependent on the circumstances in which it operated, it was perceived as something which could be negated by the functioning of the free market itself. Most frequently, monopoly was contemplated to obtain whenever a company or an allied group of companies controlled either the entire production of a commodity or a significant, though usually undefined, proportion of it. In these instances, competition had ceased to be meaningful in fact, even if it existed in theory. The trust, or the large corporation, had destroyed the freedom of the marketplace and could charge what prices it wished for the commodities it had monopolized, especially if they were "necessities." Many of the reformers in the early part of this period, although not all, voiced the belief that competition, as they understood it, could be restored by breaking up the trusts; this position was especially taken up by the nonintellectual wing of the reformist movement. They were gradually forced to recognize, as Lloyd emphasized, that "cutthroat" competition had actually led to monopoly and that the disease of combination could not be cured by simply treating the symptoms. Those practices of commerce which led to the formation of large combines were the cause of the monopolization that was engulfing America. Therefore, only by rooting out such methods of business could monopoly be prevented in the long run.

Nevertheless, as it became clear that consolidation would eventuate to a great extent whether or not certain practices were outlawed, that "monopoly" could not be averted without calling a halt to all industrial endeavor, and that combination was greatly more efficient than "competition," the opponents of the consolidation of industry altered their views, in fact if not in theory. They accepted reluctantly the industrial concentration that had come about, propounding that it was subject to regulation. Because those who did not look askance at the growth of industry also insisted that there were practices injurious to the national welfare, the differences between the fervent advocates and critics of monopoly were more semantic than real. Moreover, the Sherman Antitrust Act (1890) did not prohibit combination as such, only the attempt to "restrain trade." The transition from William Jennings Bryan, who proposed that monopoly be severely curtailed, and Louis D. Brandeis, who attacked the "curse" of bigness and demanded that illegal trusts be dissolved and the formation of new ones be prevented, to Wilson is fully illustrative of the degree to which the adversaries of the trusts changed the substance of their position. Although Wilson lambasted unjust competition, which had made it possible for the strong to crush the weak, and pressed for its abolition, he did not stand for the complete eradication of large business, as Roosevelt claimed, nor did he engage in any action to that end after becoming president. Because Roosevelt himself believed that certain trusts had to be broken up, the differences that did exist between them revolved more around the definition of "unfair" practices and the specific treatment which was to be meted out to monopoly. In essence, those who looked favorably on the trusts were able to turn the tables on their erstwhile antagonists by stressing the long-term effects of regulation, thereby portraying "socialization" as a supplement to competition, not its negation.[21]

The consensus that finally emerged was basically a victory for those who all along had argued that large-scale enterprise was inevitable and that it was to be viewed as a convenient tool for the attainment of social ends, not indiscriminately condemned. Although free exchange was rejected largely in terms duplicating the critiques, if not all the conclusions, of Ward, Bellamy, and Lloyd, the Sherman Act was to be interpreted "reasonably." The democratizing of the market was found to involve a potpourri of measures: enforcing competition by law, outlawing "predatory" practices, regulating large corporations or breaking them up as necessity dictated, nationalizing certain businesses, and conferring on the state the power to regulate prices, wages, and profits, determining who would compete with whom and on what terms. These ideas found representation in the writings of a great many writers, among whom especially may be mentioned Ely, Clark, Roosevelt, Van Hise, Weyl, Croly (who actually favored repeal of the Sherman Act), and Lippmann, who even defended the clubbing of scabs as essential to the achievement of industrial democracy.[22]

Summing up, it must be emphasized that in the deliberations of those who excoriated unhampered freedom of enterprise, the pragmatist note was thoroughly dominant. Evaluating competition and related concepts by their effects, reformers found grievous fault with many of the practices and results of the market. Particularly, one of the most prevalent, if mistaken, notions was the belief that the exchange price in many instances was somehow a distortion, not truly reflecting the value of the product in question. The reasoning employed was that if a given business had faced more competition than it actually did and had not engaged in certain methods of commerce which eliminated some rivals and discouraged potential entrants into the field, the market price would have been lower. Such was perhaps the case, but by the same norm, the prices charged by almost any business were too high, for hypothetical competition could always be envisaged which would lower the cost of many articles. In truth, no fully elaborated, let alone systematically vindicated, theory was advanced indicating how many competitors were appropriate in a given line of production.

One final point remains to be made. The exasperating vagaries of the pertinent concepts involved, such as monopoly, restraint of trade, "just" prices, and competition actually made the power of government greater in fact than it was on paper. Few progressives furnished cogent definitions of these terms, and the Sherman Antitrust Act did not elucidate the meaning of "restraint of trade."[23] Consequently, the laws controlling industry were basically fluid and could be construed in a myriad of ways. In a very real sense, any industrial achievement of whatever size could constitute a restraint of trade in that it discouraged competition, resulted in giving a larger percentage of the market to its authors, and constructed a base for further development. The murkiness of the idea of monopoly made it possible for the rule of law to be overturned, investing the bureaucracy with wide discretionary powers in regulating business for undefined ends. The most disturbing aspect of the antitrust laws, and one quite in keeping with the dynamic social-oriented spirit of the period, was not that they were heralded in the name of democratically "promoting" competition, however illusory such a notion might be, but that they released government from the bondage of indicating precisely which acts were illegal.

Now it would have been quite possible to pass a specific law to prevent such mergers [of two or more corporations]; all that was necessary was to limit their charters, and forbid one corporation to buy another, or any shares in it. Such a law might have been either senseless or somewhat harmful: it would certainly have been in restraint of trade, but the political power is restrictive; and the law would have been specific in naming the act proscribed . . . That was the one thing the legislators would not do . . . Their object was to secure control of the corporations. It was attained by using a phrase which could be construed as covering any business transaction whatever.[24]

Moreover, given the ambiguity suffusing "monopoly," it is understandable that even those who originally sought to regulate only it finally arrived, by assuming that competition was equivalent to beneficial effects, at the position that all property was liable to state control. In any case, the Sherman Act was made to serve as the primary instrument by which the state "corrected" competition and supervised the market.

All in all, the collectivist concept of democracy helped break down the "artificial" separation of politics and society, making the former a servant of the latter. Constraints on popular rule, denounced as undemocratic, were to be removed. Therefore, attention was shifted, as Wilson had observed, from the study of political structure to the examination of the anatomy of society. Social relationships were now scrutinized for autocratic elements. Wherever such elements were found, the rule of the people was to be applied to rectify the situation. And because society was constantly and rather unpredictably changing, the law, both constitutional and nonconstitutional, had to be interpreted flexibly, in accordance with the needs of the times. Democracy, hitherto defined in purely political terms, had been fully "socialized."

The numerous theories of democratizing the market, however, did not supply that comprehensive framework required for reform. It was the social interest, in all its variants, that occupied the central place in this schema. A consideration of this filter that transformed claims into rights is crucial to the understanding of the collectivism espoused by the progressives.

CHAPTER VI

EMPIRICAL COLLECTIVISM

The overall character of progressive thought was manifested in the complete abandonment of the outlook of early republicanism. The actual policy prescriptions proffered by reform-minded intellectuals, as well as the justifications they adduced for them, were set forth in a context basically alien to that in which republicans couched their analysis. Again, progressives, fascinated by the vision of a reified society evolving in time, substituted social for political concepts. Of primary importance to them was the study of society in all its multitudinous aspects. They derived sweeping political conclusions from sociological premises and found the subject matter of politics, not in politics itself, but in a formidable matrix of social phenomena. This departure from the orientation of republican individualism enabled reformers to perceive the state as a legitimate purveyor of concrete social interests and to raise no objection in principle to a general regulation of trade and industry. Society could now work its will through political organs.

In broad essentials, the doctrines of progressives can be characterized as both collectivist and empirical. With reference to the former, the central meaning of the social interest was that it completely subordinated the individual to the community, leaving no sphere open to him in which he could function by right. With regard to the latter, there was a quite consciously elaborated rebellion against theory. Critics of the limited state sought to examine actual social processes subject to sensory verification, not the convolutions of the Absolute. From this antitheoretical bias resulted an endorsement of, and prescription for, a gradual, pragmatic socialization, one disdaining abstract principles. The empiricism of reformers, then, consisted in their fact-oriented approach, not necessarily in the truth of their observations.

Early republican theorists had employed the term "public interest" frequently, if with some vagueness. They did not apply it to refer to the interests of a supraindividual entity. Nor did they regard it as endowing government with indefinite powers over persons and property. On the contrary, because government was instituted for specific objects, the interests of the public were not all-encompassing. Instead, they pertained only to a carefully, constitutionally delimited sphere given content by the conception of natural rights common to all individuals. There was, therefore, a definite, private realm with which the state could not interfere. Government was rigidly limited in its scope and prevented from acting "arbitrarily" by the powers clearly enumerated in the Constitution. The public interest, as Madison and others were eager to point out, did not confer additional functions upon the rulers beyond those stated.

Reformers transmuted the public good into the "social interest," a phrase for which they exhibited a marked predilection. In so doing, they entirely changed its meaning. Although they still recognized the common good as the criterion by which governmental action was to be adjudged, they maintained that the public sphere could not be restricted by metaphysical theories of innate rights. On the contrary, because the polity had to respond docilely to the social will, there could be no other conceivable limitation on the power of the government than the needs of society. The dependence of the political upon the social, then, made it impossible to posit the existence of two autonomous spheres functioning independently of each other. Through the grace of the social interest, government, no longer bound by a written enumeration of its powers, was free to act as it wished, taking on any function that might be deemed socially expedient.

This paramountcy of society did not mean merely that the traditional idea of obligation was overthrown, a new one substituted, and capital portrayed as a communal product. The gravest of errors would be to make the entirely chimerical supposition that rights were simply "redefined" and made effective on a different plane, the individual being conceded some sort of sphere of action, presumably in a "social" context, immune to the collectivity's interference. Equally mistaken would be the assumption that some forms of human activity inherently lay outside the scope of the "new rights." Quite to the contrary, the corollary plainly drawn was that control of all property was to be invested in the collective, that individual effort was to be directed in accordance with the exigencies of the national welfare, and that society, employing whatever instrumentalities at its disposal, including the state, would decide what was to be produced, how it was to be produced, and to whom the goods were to be distributed. The key characteristic of the social interest, all verbiage aside, turned out to be the denial of any right to property. This interpretation of the social welfare was completely in harmony with the expansive concept of monopoly which most reformers ended up approving.

Such a notion was advanced explicitly by a number of writers and was implicit in the expositions of countless others. Perhaps Theodore Roosevelt most frankly and lucidly presented it when he insisted that the "right to regulate the use of wealth in the public interest is universally admitted" and called for the similar supervision of labor, noting that every person must be given the opportunity to make the "greatest possible contribution to the public welfare." It was also directly expressed in Edward A. Ross's contrasting of public welfare and the quest for profit, Westel Willoughby's "enlightened utilitarianism" which "subordinated individual interests to the general weal of the community," and Richard Ely's social theory of property acquisition and use. It was no less to be found in Lester Ward's claim that the state, "the organ of social consciousness," could use any means to achieve the common good, Justice Waite's depiction of property as "clothed with a public interest," and the lucubrations of most sociologists who, in the words of Barnes, came to the conclusion that the "social interest is the only limitation which can be placed upon state activity and the only criterion by which it can be adequately guided." Walter Weyl's determination that society alone could decide "what things may be produced and how" and his declaration that the "sovereign state has a primordial, intrinsic, underlying right to all property, more valid in the final instance than the property rights vested in the legal owner" were in the same spirit.[1]

Most emphatically, the ideology of reformers was not a mean between free industry and collectivism. In actual practice, the economy was not fully "socialized" in the sense of being made completely subject to controls. What emerged was a mixture of free enterprise and governmental regulation. In theory, however, all property was potentially liable to the control of the state. If certain economic transactions were left uncontrolled, it was not because of intrinsic right. Rather, the social interest presumably was being served in the absence of regulation. What freedom of action as did exist was contingent upon its continued utility to the wants of the public. If individual initiative in a given area no longer produced the desired results, then the state would step in and prescribe the rules that would ensure that the social interest was promoted. In sum, the shift from the public good, conceived as referring to an autonomous political sphere delimited by the enumeration of governmental powers, to the social good, envisaged as the attribute of an inherently illimitable entity, culminated in the destruction of the barriers that republicans had established between politics and society. Because the state, acting in the name of society, was now invested with broad, nonspecific power over life and property, an innately private area of action, based on contractual arrangements, could not exist.

At this point, the question may be legitimately posed as to whether the doctrines put forth by progressives were "socialistic." In so far as socialism is considered in its narrow, or orthodox, meaning, the answer must be in the negative. Many reformers did insist that what they were advocating was essentially socialism. Richard T. Ely, for instance, asserted that he was in sympathy with a general form of it, one which, he noted, had been expounded by most outstanding thinkers.

Socialism in this large sense frequently has reference, in a general way, to the views and aspirations of those who hold that the individual should subordinate himself to society, maintaining that thus alone can the welfare of all be secured. Socialism in this more general sense implies the rejection of the doctrine of selfishness as a sufficient social force and the affirmation of altruism as a principle of social action. Socialism, in this broad sense of the word, means that society is not a mere aggregation of individuals, but a living, growing organism, the laws of which are something different from the laws of individual action.

And Walter Rauschenbusch, a leading figure in the Social Gospel movement, maintained that he supported "practical socialism."[2] Moreover, the writings of orthodox socialists, many of whom saw progressivism as a road to the achievement of their goals,[3] did exert a formidable impact on the ideology of reformers.[4]

Still, even when progressives described their position as one of socialism, they were always quick to qualify it by such adjectives as "broad," "practical," or "general," among others. In fact, American collectivism differed from classical socialism, as it had originated in Europe, in several important ways. Most American proponents of the "positive state" (Edward Bellamy being the major exception) did not advocate that all the means of production and all property be directly taken over by government. Nationalization was occasionally suggested, especially as a remedy for the bugbear of monopoly; yet it was regarded as unnecessary in most instances. Moreover, the proximate and long-range interests of society, not those of the proletariat, were postulated as the criteria by which reforms were to be judged.[5] Even when the living conditions of a class or a specific group of men were improved, the guiding consideration was said to be the good of society as a whole. The benefits that were to be distributed were to be allocated in accordance with the requirements of society, and the community itself was to act as the agent of change, not a particular class. In addition, most reformers repudiated class war.[6] Many believed as well that socialist schemes were, in the nature of things, impracticable.[7] Perhaps the most pervasive criticism voiced, however, was that socialism was too theoretical and did not take account of actual conditions. Lester Ward, for instance, denied the validity of the belief that the government should nationalize the whole of industry; he felt that the arguments adduced for it were inadequate "chiefly because they have consisted so largely of pure theory and a priori deductions." From a similar perspective, Herbert Croly took to task both traditional individualism and socialism for conceiving of "their specific programs, their immediate itineraries, as an adequate and a safe guide-book for the entire journey," noting that progressive democracy had to abandon the "illusion of any such assurance." And Walter Weyl criticized socialism as too theoretical, dogmatic, and absolute, observing that its categorical predictions had been falsified by history.[8] Thus, although American collectivism continued to underscore the subordination of the individual to the community, it did not find in socialism an adequate alternative to free government.

What, then, was the content of the progressive ideology? What practical actions were to be taken by the state to further the interests of the community? Reformers always avowed that the social interest was the guiding criterion for legislation. However, determining the substantive nature of the policies that should be followed was hampered by the difficulty of visualizing an entity embodying "all of the people" and devising a program of action based on its corporeality. American democratic collectivism was able to overcome this problem by adopting a militantly empirical standpoint, one which elevated experience at the expense of theory. The social interest was to be given content in terms of the facts.

With the exception of some of the early critics of free government, theory was constantly deprecated through this period. Even Brownson and Mulford had made frequent references to the emptiness of dead abstractions, particularly as they manifested themselves in formal institutions and the written constitution. Nevertheless, there was no general attack on theory as such, although the implication of the "dynamic" view of the nation was obviously antitheoretical. In many ways, the publication of Henry George's *Progress and Poverty* in 1879 marked the caesura between the early, idealistic-oriented criticism and the later, "practical" criticism, with its conspicuous disdain for abstractions. George's own work was both a vindication of theory and a rejection of it. He affirmed the system of natural rights and held that men ought to be guided by it in their organization of society. But at the same time he maintained that the right to property, interpreted in an abstract sense, led to its own negation, as indicated by the great disparity in wealth. Still, his panacea focused on one measure, making the state universal landlord, and did not contemplate a constant series of adjustments and readjustments to an elusive reality.

Those who followed George disparaged theory because they believed that concepts could not capture the essence of reality. They imagined that society was in a state of flux, continually developing, and that explicitly formulated and rigorously exact theories were of little utility in understanding human action. A concept had reference to some entity or an attribute of an entity; consequently, it was static in its orientation. A theory was a combination of concepts purporting to explain certain phenomena and to prescribe a course of action appropriate to the facts. Because it disregarded the change that so manifestly characterized reality, it could claim, at best, only limited validity. Those aspects of reality which had given rise to the concepts in question had altered even as they were being generalized into abstractions. Indeed, it was often claimed that a concept could never refer to a definite thing and that only processes, not objects, existed. As some critics attested, one logical conclusion of pragmatism was not only that one could not step in the same river twice, but that one could not even do it once.

Grand abstractions were denigrated, therefore, as a tool for the prehension of existence. Theories based on absolutes, such as free government or socialism, were merely ideologies bearing no discernible relation to the problems of men other than an aspiration or a pretense at solving them. The ideals to be found in them were often not subject to experiential verification, and when they were, the means advocated were not germane to the ends posited. Thus, with free production and exchange, unlimited competition resulted in unrestricted monopoly, and the right to property entailed the enrichment of a few at the expense of the many, instead of guaranteeing material possessions to all. In these instances, as in others, theory clashed with practice because it either derived its ideals from a supernatural realm or because it assumed a static universe. In the latter case, the norms involved may have been useful at one time, but if social change rendered them obsolete, the continued insistence on their "truth" would be equivalent to the assertion of an arrogant a priori proposition and would produce harm. Reality would be made to conform to absolute notions instead of serving as the ground for all reasoning.

If theory was not to guide action, what was to take its place? How could any prescriptions be advanced without recourse to theorizing of some sort? Here, the opponents of free government raised the banner of experience, positing a standard which was free from any a priori bases. Certain writers, most prominently Arthur Bentley, held this to imply an anti-intellectualistic psychology.[9] Men were not moved by ideas or thoughts but by other forces that were primary and that produced corresponding behavior patterns. Ideas, as manifested in verbal and written statements, were simply epiphenomenal, the product of these forces. In some cases, they were an adequate representation of the actual motives, while in others they were a distorted reflection of them. But no matter which, they remained secondary.

Most reformers, however, offered no explicit view of man's psychology. They assumed that abstractions were invalid and that the chosen standard was not a theoretical one. It was implied that "facts" or "effects" in themselves were sufficient to comprehend a given situation and to indicate the course of action that was to be undertaken, if any. This presumption found particular support in the writings of the founders of pragmatism, who reduced meaning to consequences. Thus, William James postulated that to test the truth of an idea, the essential point was to determine what concrete differences would result if the conception in question were assumed to be first true and then false. John Dewey claimed that reality could only be penetrated by "referring all thinking, all reflective considerations, to *consequences* for final meaning and test." Charles Peirce likewise believed that the total import of an idea could be established by examining the effects it entailed. He advised that "in order to ascertain the meaning of an intellectual conception one should consider what practical consequences might conceivably result by necessity from the truth of that conception; and the sum of these consequences will constitute the entire meaning of the conception." [10]

Most progressives adhered to this line of thinking, whether or not influenced directly by philosophical pragmatism. To them, it was impossible to predict the actual problems that would arise in the course of the nation's development and to prognosticate, or prescribe, the nature of the solutions that would be implemented. Holding narrow context to be the fundamental determinant of policy, they insisted that long-range principles providing an all-inclusive justification for action were to be eschewed. Whatever was found to be expedient or convenient was to be executed, even at the risk of seeming inconsistency. They did not argue that principles had to be applied to differing conditions and that differing prescriptions would therefore result; rather, expediency would produce a solution to the problem in question; a recourse to abstract formulas was not necessary at all. Experience would illuminate all the conceivable effects of a proposed policy, and the reformer would judge whether they were a relevant response to the problem under consideration. There was no need for theory when a mere examination of the facts was adequate.

Consequently, facts (or effects) were counterposed to theory throughout the post–Civil War period by advocates of the positive state. Woodrow Wilson found fault with those who would restrict government within narrow constitutional limits and hinder its operation as an instrument of popular will through such devices as checks and balances. He observed that the view that society was a living structure and could not be hobbled by abstract notions was "not theory, but fact, and displays its force as fact, whatever theories may be thrown across its track." Henry Demarest Lloyd, in his running attack on monopoly, continually upbraided those who, by clinging to useless abstractions, ignored the "facts" of industrial concentration. It was evident that the effects produced by hectic competition were sufficient refutation of the curious idea that monopoly could be created only by government. Walter Lippmann, adopting William James's view that a given concept should be employed only when it is of use, cautioned that any large classification "fits each single fact very badly." It was of the very nature of reality that general principles, when applied to concrete circumstances, proved to be unreliable. "The moment you act in some real situation, say in some labor dispute," he exclaimed, "your large generalizations have to undergo enormous modifications."[11]

Similarly, Thorstein Veblen railed that those who invoked theory were disregarding self-evident facts. "The endeavor is to make facts conform to law, not to make the law or general rule conform to facts. The bent so given favors the acceptance of the general, abstract, custom-made rule as something real with a reality superior to the reality of the impersonal, non-conventional facts," Lester Ward asserted that whether a proposed course of action was desirable was a "simple question of fact, and its adoption or rejection must always, as now, be due to the opinion of the legislator as to what are to be its effects." Oliver Wendell Holmes accentuated the role of experience in the making of the law. "General propositions do not decide concrete cases. The decision will depend on a judgment or intuition more subtle than any articulate major premise." Roscoe Pound noted that the "sociological jurists" looked more to the working of the law than to its abstract content. They regarded legal precepts as mere guides to socially just results, not inflexible molds. American courts had acted unrealistically when they held to "rigorous logical deductions from predetermined conceptions in disregard of and often in the teeth of the actual facts" Perhaps Frank Goodnow summed it up best when, taking cognizance of the decline of the ideas of natural rights and the social contract, he wrote that "at the present time thoughtful men are coming more and more to the conviction that a static society is all but impossible and that absolute political ideals are incapable of realization. More and more political and social students are recognizing that a policy of opportunism is the policy most likely to be followed by desirable results and that adherence to general theories which are to be applied at all times and under all conditions is productive of harm rather than good."[12]

The ramifications of this empiricism were rather far-reaching. One immediate consequence was that American collectivism was marked by an extensive ambiguity. The exaltation of expediency meant that specific policies could not be deduced from general principles, only from the needs of the moment. Hence, the sum of all the measures taken in all the individual cases appeared to be a farrago lacking any kind of unity. Indeed, many reformers proudly announced that they had no long-range program of action.[13] The antidoctrinal character of the progressive ideology was expressed by the ever ingenuous Walter Weyl when he wrote that socialization was "less a definite industrial program than the animating ideal of a whole industrial policy."[14]

A more fundamental consequence was that the system of free exchange was found to be incompatible with the facts. Those who criticized it repeatedly contended that it had frequently failed in practice, adducing case after case in which it had proved disastrous without specifying the criterion by which success and failure were judged. Economist Irving Fisher, trying to explain why laissez-faire had been discarded, proposed that its "abandonment has been gradual and almost unconscious, not so much the result of any rival abstract doctrine, as the cumulative effect of experience." In hundreds of cases, he maintained, "socialistic" measures had been enacted to correct the deficiencies of the free market. Walter Lippmann discovered that a problem existed whenever private wealth was not devoted to the best interests of the nation.

"Could the government make better use of Mr. Carnegie's hugh fortune than Mr. Carnegie does?—that is the problem. Are there better uses to which it might be put than those which Mr. Carnegie has in mind? If there are, then the government is entirely justified in substituting itself for Mr. Carnegie as a dispenser of libraries and peace palaces." Roscoe Pound lamented that the American judiciary clung to the outmoded conceptions of contract and equality of rights "in the face of notorious social and economic facts." The implication was that a value complex was inherent in the facts, one which could easily be recognized. Any reliance on theory was unnecessary and undesirable. A given situation should be scrutinized in isolation, the relevant aspects of reality noted, and a plan of action submitted which would produce the beneficial effects so ardently sought. The facts were sufficient to indicate whether something had to be done and what had to be done, without the meddling mediation of troublesome abstractions. The extent to which this view had permeated the culture and had even gained acceptance by its ostensible opponents, was revealed in the case of the Oregon law limiting the hours women could work. The Supreme Court ruled that the law was constitutional, supporting Louis Brandeis's brief on behalf of the state, in which he argued that the facts supported a limitation on the working day. Only two pages of his 104-page brief were devoted to general legal considerations; the rest discussed conditions.[15] The intimation was that a mere iteration of the facts was satisfactory proof of the undesirability of these conditions and the necessity for their alleviation, not the advancement of general theory.

But even the gathering and description of "facts" is a conceptual operation, not something which occurs automatically upon the application of mind to reality. Observers may come to different conclusions as to what the facts are. There is no guarantee that disputes will not arise. Facts are propositions, conveyed in either oral or written terms and, consequently, do not constitute an experience somehow divorced from concepts.[16] Moreover, to ascertain whether a problem exists or whether certain actions are beneficial or harmful requires a code of values. Experience may well teach what effects can be expected from the implementation of a policy. The evaluation of them is a normative process. Many of the pragmatist constructs, such as those of "facts" and "problem," actually concealed value premises despite disclaimers to the contrary. The clothing of value judgments in the supposedly neutral garb of experience made it possible to depict certain courses of action as flowing ineluctably from the nature of the facts. Progressives seldom acknowledged the distinction between fact and value, nor did they admit that describing both the observed problem and its solution required a consideration of fundamental values. As a result, they often avoided an axiological discussion. Moreover, this concentration on the immediate consequences narrowed the range in which an alleged problem was analyzed, so that broader implications and the larger context were ignored. Once it was possible to make one's ideological adversary accept the facts, it was only a matter of time before he was led to concede the appropriate solution.[17]

Implicit values of a rather diverse sort played a crucial role, then, in the treatment of various issues. Whether a result was to be construed as desirable depended upon the personal values of the reformer. Herbert Croly, for instance, brought to his analysis of the "labor problem" a preconceived aversion to nonunion labor, denouncing it as "industrial derelict." It was to be rejected, for unions deserved "frank and legal support." Although only good unions should be recognized, they alone were to be allowed to establish employment for their members; the closed shop was necessary. Moreover, the government was also to ensure that workers were paid a "fair minimum wage." It is understandable, given such predilections, that when it was discovered that nonunion workers were competing with unionized labor or that employees were not obtaining a "fair" recompense for their services, a difficulty was triumphantly discerned through mere recitation of the "facts." In like fashion, Walter Weyl excoriated the market economy for producing what he alluded to as "useless" articles. It was also distinguished by a senseless duplication of plant and product. Regulation of industry, Weyl felt, would put an end to this situation.[18] Here again, personal values occupied a prominent place in the reasoning. Something that may be useful to one man may not be so to another. By insisting on the "fact" that certain commodities were inherently unessential, despite market demand for them, and could thus be dispensed with, Weyl was projecting a value judgment into his analysis.

Other progressives similarly introduced, largely tacitly, ethical premises into their arguments. They often spoke of the need for a "living" wage or of "noxious" industrial practices,[19] insinuating that the existence of such phenomena proved the desirability for remedial action by the state. Now, the value to which they gave the greatest emphasis, and to which other values were often seen as instrumental, was equality. Over and over again, they analyzed conditions and detected baneful inequalities; solutions were then offered to lessen the disparities in question. Equality in many cases did function as the criterion by which effects were appraised.

American collectivists not only gave content to the general welfare by concentrating on facts perceived to obtain in exiguously defined situations. They also focused on the actual interests constituting the social environment in which the political system reputedly functioned. Social facts were found to consist of social forces. The meaning of the repeated assertion that the state was a tool of society now becomes clear. The government was to be made to serve as the vehicle by which socioeconomic groups would advance their welfare, even if at the expense of the rest of the population and even if property were redistributed by law. Republicans, of course, had not denied that "interests" of a socioeconomic nature existed, believing that legislation which tended to achieve the good of all sections of the community was desirable as long as the rights of men were not violated. Yet, one object of republican theorizing had been to devise arrangements that would make it impossible for social groups to use political organs for their own, special ends. It was presumed that the various groups should promote their well-being largely within a system of free contract. Retreating from the political orientation of republicanism, reformers spurned this view, advocating unlimited majority rule and reducing politics to the struggle of interests for the control of the state. The reality of government was now manifested in the social processes by which the community arrived at its decisions.

By and large, critics of free government in the early part of this period did not explicitly engage in group analysis. Their treatment of the polity, however, also was reductionist, empirically condensing social forces into general tendencies and picturing the state as a mirror of societal trends. For instance, Edward Bellamy, whose thought was acutely characteristic in this respect, took a rather holistic approach. Although he did not divide the population into separate economic strata, he denied the autonomy of politics just as much as the theorists of groups did. Essentially, he projected the image of a homogeneous society (as he perceived it) into government, making of the latter a similitude of the former. Social developments established a decisive example for the political system. Bellamy came to the conclusion that the primary "fact" characterizing free competition was that it led to increasing consolidation, so that the point would finally be reached when one large syndicate controlled the production of all goods. This situation, which solved the labor problem, came about as a resultant of a "process of industrial evolution," society merely recognizing and cooperating with that evolution "when its tendency had become unmistakable." Private control of this giant trust for personal profit was abolished, for society took it over directly, managing the "common interest for the common profit." Bellamy did not envision the destruction of the state, making it clear that it was government acting as an arm of society which forcibly dispossessed the former owners of private industry, ensured economic equality, and directed production. Still, if the state was not abolished, it was devalued as an autonomous agency. Bellamy's analysis centered around the structure of society. He drew his political conclusions as inferences from social data and, generally speaking, gave little explicit treatment of governmental organs. He expressed this supplantation of political by social categories in a number of ways. First, the state was now patterned on society itself. The nation, conducted as "one great business corporation," became the single capitalist. The component parts of this corporation were guilds, or syndicates, which controlled the production of selected commodities. Second, because society had absorbed the polity, the "stuff of politics" had radically changed. Although Congress still existed, there was virtually no legislation. And most of the functions for which government had been instituted, with the exception of those pertaining to the judiciary and the police, were no longer being exercised. These developments had been brought about by the aboliton of private property. Because "fully ninety-nine hundreths of the laws" of nineteenth-century America concerned its "definition and protection" and the "relations of buyers and sellers," the appropriation of private property by society obviated the need for extensive legislation.[20]

Lester Ward was less holistic in his approach, and also less specific, than Bellamy. He called neither for the entire ownership of industry by the government nor for complete equality of incomes. Additionally, the facts that he observed were of a different character. Instead of discovering a single, ineluctable trend toward a monolithic consolidation, he, like the great majority of democratic collectivists, perceived a plurality of factors combining in a complex fashion. Society was still an organic whole, yet one whose "parts" could be studied. "Society is simply a compound organism whose acts exhibit the resultant of all the individual forces which its members exert. These acts, whether individual or collective, obey fixed laws. Objectively viewed, society is a natural object, presenting a variety of complicated movements produced by a particular class of natural forces." Such natural forces, Ward thought, were preeminently social in nature and consisted, therefore, of human desire or feeling. Although intelligence, or reason, could direct them, they propelled society along its path, a fact which had to accepted as a given by the philosopher.[21]

Ward maintained that the state existed to minister to the needs of society and that the latter was composed of social forces struggling to attain their goals. If these premises are accepted, it logically follows that government must seek to maximize the satisfaction of human desires, whatever they may inhere in. What this meant in practice was that the state could rightfully be employed to better the position of certain interests at the expense of others. With constitutional safeguards on majority rule removed, it became the prize to be won in a social contest. Ward's theory of attractive legislation was a statement of this whole position. Sociocracy would inquire into the interests of society and would fix laws inducing men to act for the public good by making it advantageous for the individual to do that which was beneficial for the community. Government had done harm in the past, not because of any innate difficulties inherent in state intervention, but because of a lack of knowledge, which would be remedied by the unveiling of the social forces through the science of society. Ward, obliterating the distinction between force and freedom, explained that "attractive legislation" would mean the lessening of the repressive functions of government. For example, it would lower the rates of the telegraph and of other goods in general, actions that were in the interest of society and that would be opposed only by an "interested few." Tariffs, bounties, and other subsidies would also redound to the public welfare and were ways of encouraging, rather than restricting, human action.[22] The whole thrust of Ward's theory of attractive legislation amounted, then, to sanctioning the use of the state to satisfy "human desires" by redistributing income, either through the taxing power or the regulation of industry. The measures that Ward proposed might, indeed, have encouraged human activity; in fact, in some cases they might even have created "social forces." Yet, such incentives for action could be brought into play only by making the state a purveyor of wealth.

Those who followed Lester Ward built on the foundations he had laid. They, as well, denied the autonomy of politics. But they moved beyond Ward by fathoming that behind the social forces lay a plurality of interest associations. Their empiricism centered around both the existence of groups and the interaction among them. Just as with Ward, the concept of the social interest was not thereby discarded but rather given concrete content. This was another manifestation of collective subjectivism; the truth was a process in which the community made known its will. Such a process inhered in the bargaining procedures by which conflicting desires were adjusted. "Problems" were solved, in so far as all germane claims were reconciled. The compromise of interests came to constitute the experience of the community. The social interest, then, designated the actual outcome produced by the contending of the sundry groups that composed society.

Roscoe Pound maintained that interests lay behind the idea of right. He held that claims should be evaluated by the standard of the social interest, feeling that the granting of reasonable demands was to the advantage of the community. Still, he believed that an individual was being "reasonable" whenever he reconciled his desires, whatever they were, with those of others. "More and more the tendency is to hold that what the law should secure is satisfaction of the owner's reasonable wants with respect to the property—that is, those which consist with the like wants of his neighbors and with the interests of society." Although he always insisted that interests were not being balanced against one another but weighed to see how and to what extent they accorded with the general good, in the spirit of "democracy" he advanced a utilitarian precept for dealing with the myriad of claims. The end of law, he reasoned, is "the satisfaction of as many human demands as we can with the least sacrifice of other demands."[23] Yet, because the state could obviously not satisfy all demands, and therefore had to sanction only those deemed reasonable, Pound's criterion effectively meant that the struggle of interests, amounting to the adjustment of desires, would determine the general welfare.

Democratic collectivists, such as Weyl, Lippmann, and Bentley, expressly legitimized interest group conflict, emphasizing the paramount role of pragmatic bargaining in the framing of legislation. All were rather eclectic in their approach. Weyl looked forward to a gradual socialization stemming from class coalitions and compromises. It would involve governmental regulation and ownership of industry, tax reform, and a variety of measures designed to improve the standard of living. Deploring class warfare, Weyl called for the peaceful struggle of groups to give substance to the public good. Walter Lippmann prophesied that labor, capital, and consumer interests would vie among themselves, the demands of the last destined to be the strongest. Businessmen would be converted into public servants, and unions would be endowed with considerable power. The ultimate result of the contest among the various socioeconomic strata would be a form of state socialism, controlling property through public ownership and regulation.[24]

Arthur Bentley gave the most sophisticated and lengthy treatment of interest groups. He adopted an anti-intellectualistic psychology which held that ideas were secondary to actual behavior (hence, his persistent stress on "process"). Regarding activity, not as a product of a group, but as identical to it, he considered it as prior to ideation. "Indeed the only reality of the ideas is their reflection of the groups, only that and nothing more. The ideas can be stated in terms of the groups, the groups never in terms of the ideas." The entire population could be divided into groups, all of which have interests, although not always economic in character. Bentley vouchsafed that the operation of interest groups accounted for all political phenomena. "When the groups are adequately stated, everything is stated. When I say everything I mean everything." The essence of politics revealed itself as interest associations bargaining over the resources of the community. Moreover, one of the fundamental characteristics of the process of group interaction was compromise.[25] All in all, Bentley regarded the state as derivative, as one tool, albeit an important one, by which social forces, in the form of groups, worked their will. Whatever consensus obtained was valid, for it reflected the experience of the collectivity. Any "checks" on state authority could arise only through the very contesting of the interests themselves. Once again, the rejection of the independence of the political sector culminated in the denial of the existence of the two spheres posited by republican constitutionalism.

Other reformers, toward the close of this era, added virtually nothing to these views. They, too, conceived of groups as the essential claimants to the social product. And they imagined pragmatic bargaining and compromise to be the crux of the interplay of interests. Admittedly, their interpretations of the "facts" often differed; they agreed, nevertheless, that a truly empirical approach necessitated that political phenomena be studied as one aspect of the processes brought about by the warfare of a multitude of social forces. The general welfare, no longer regarded as defining a separate governmental sphere, came to signify the actual result arrived at by society. From this perspective alone, all antitheoretical prejudices aside, it is clear that its composition could not be rigorously specified, for the simple reason that no long-range principles were capable of being established when the phantasmogoric contest among diverse groups, the give-and-take that occurred over the community's resources, could produce virtually any outcome.

The empiricism of American collectivism, whether in its guise of focusing upon facts in a restricted context or that of concentrating upon groups, had two additional consequences. First, one product of the revolt against doctrine was the impoverishment of political theory. Not a single outstanding political theorist emerged in this period. Indeed, the science of government became a kind of applied sociology. Writers on politics simply echoed the views of sociologists and economists[26] and contributed little from the theoretical viewpoint. The state became one of the many avenues by which society attained its goals. The polity was now regarded as a subsystem of a more generic social system. It followed logically that political theory, not having a body of doctrine of its own, had to adapt sociological theorems to its specific subject matter. Therefore, an investigation of government required a preliminary, pertinacious, and intensive analysis of the forces that molded social relationships.

There were hardly any works which offered a fundamental treatment of the nature and origin of the state. What general theorizing as was produced was aimed at proving the superfluity of theory. This situation especially prevailed toward the close of the period, when the pragmatist trend had become dominant. Consequently, many of the most crucial issues were considered in a constricted rather than a broad framework, with no reference to theoretical principles. This was true even before groups were discovered to be the major factor in the political process. Economic monographs dealing with specific problems, such as the publications of the American Economic Association, and sociological tracts, such as the works of Ward, Small, and Cooley, replaced the political treatise. Even the few democratic collectivists who wrote extensively on the state openly repudiated theory and conceded their dependence on sociology. Willoughby, for instance, frankly discarded theory and acknowledged that his arguments against laissez-faire simply reproduced those of Ward.[27]

The decline of political theory was manifested especially by the oft-made declaration that the state had to be accepted as something self-evident, that it was futile to question its existence.[28] This position eliminated the central and abiding concern of political philosophy, namely, the etiology and function of the state. It was, in part, intended to refute the criticism of those who wished to place all issues in a theoretical perspective and analyze "problems" in terms of fundamentals, proceeding acropetally, moving from the base, the first principles, to the apex, derivative abstractions and applied premises. The shrinking of context, the concentrating on the state's function in a particular case and not in general, was a product of the empirical orientation of pragmatic collectivism and was conductive to smuggling in implicit premises. Moreover, many writers evinced the same tendencies when discussing the nature of the functions that the state was to assume. They urged that intervention of the government in economic affairs had to be taken as a given, that it could not be questioned on theoretical grounds. The only choice lay in the precise character of that intervention. Almost all submitted that free industry had become pragmatically equivalent to discrimination in favor of a few and that only actual legislation in behalf of the masses could effect some kind of balance, distributing benefits more generally. They frequently adduced this argument to prove the worthlessness of theory and to undermine the counterclaims of those intent upon making distinctions between the power of government and the "power" acquired in the free market. They scrutinized the past, including that of America, and the actual behavior of governments to show that the state had always intervened and that it was therefore puerile to insist that it could not, for the collective experience of mankind as embodied in such intervention was superior to the whimsical emanations of an individual consciousness.

Hence, Chief Justice Waite, in his decision in *Munn* v. *Illinois*, pronounced that Congress had regulated certain prices and rates before the Civil War and that such regulation had not been considered unconstitutional. Woodrow Wilson distinguished between constituent and ministrant functions of the state, defining the former as that class which was essential to the preservation of life, liberty, and property and the latter as those which advanced the general interests of society. Constituent functions were necessary even under the strictest minimizing of the role of the state, Wilson observed, whereas ministrant functions, including the regulation of labor and industry, care of the poor and incapable, education, and internal improvements, were optional. The latter, however, although lying in the domain of expediency, had been undertaken by all governments alike in one form or another.[29] The intimation was that because this was the case and had always been the case, any theory attempting to divest the state of the right to legislate in the "general interests of society" ran counter to the wisdom of mankind, acquired over the ages. Consequently, it was a quixotic effort to subject reality to abstractions. Other critics of free exchange pointed out that defenders of the limited state were quite willing to support certain abridgments of contract by the political authorities and to tolerate the confiscation of property for certain "public" purposes. A pure form of free industry had never existed in America, or anywhere else for that matter.

Frank Goodnow, pursuing this line of thought, stated that from a very early point in our history, taxation for the support of the poor had existed, despite the rule forbidding the taking of property for anything but public purpose. Defending intervention not on the basis of abstract considerations but on past experience, he noted that certain acts of the government unjustifiable in terms of a strict construction of the Constitution had been accepted as a matter of course. Hence, to those who say that the "granting of old age, sickness and accident pensions is an unwarrantable extension of the activity of the federal government it may be answered that such action is no more of an extension of that activity than the grant of bounties for the encouragement of manufacturing which is subject to state rather than to federal regulation, or than the grant of money to educational institutions, which is provided by the Morrell act [*sic*], or the gratuitous distribution of seeds to farmers." Goodnow, visualizing the general welfare as something other than a tag for enumerated powers, fastened a collectivist meaning onto it, one supposedly vindicated by the history of its interpretation, however limited state intervention may actually have been. He claimed that neither the right to property nor the Constitution could restrict the right of the legislature to enforce the public good. "Who in view of the history of the public domain will venture to say that the constitution limits the power of Congress to dispose of the public funds as it sees fit in order to promote what it considers to be the 'public welfare of the United States' to provide for which the constitution specifically says the taxing power may be used?"[30]

Thus, progressives took the history of intervention by the state in both the processes of production and distribution and generalized it into part of the American experience. They conceived of the public welfare as an attribute of "society as a whole." By writing off this country's substantial record of nonintervention and citing instead the practices of other nations, they were able to descant on intervention as a question of fact, not one of theory, and rebuke their adversaries for impudently bringing metaphysics into the discussion. Ignoring the warnings of Madison and Paine not to take precedents out of context, reformers concluded that, in evolutionary fashion, state intervention had been consistently growing and would continue to grow, not taking into account whether the intervention in question was strictly constitutional, consonant with property rights, or justifiable for specific, assignable reasons.

The second consequence of the empiricism of American collectivism was that the power of the state could not be rigorously delimited. The functions that the state was to undertake could only be ascertained by an investigation of all the factors germane to a particular situation. Because conditions varied and because society was in a constant state of flux, it would be impossible to establish a general standard to which the actions of government had to conform in advance. Consequently, each point at issue had to be appraised separately and its strengths and weaknesses weighed in the balance. Strict constitutional interpretation was undesirable, for it was an attempt to constrain the exercise of power and to prescribe in advance what was and was not permitted. This pragmatic view of state functions was often contrasted with those theories, such as free government and socialism, which settled exactly what the state was to do in all instances.

Woodrow Wilson, adhering to this notion, explicated that, with respect to ministrant functions, there were few differences among countries, for *"government does now whatever experience permits or the times demand."* Edmund James, in his interesting study of the gas supply, wrote that government functions could not be determined a priori and that in the case of gas, a necessity of life, the chaos of private enterprise had made public ownership desirable. Charles Cooley held that the sphere of government could not be fixed and that it varied with social conditions. "Hard-and-fast theories of what the state may best be and do, whether restrictive or expansive, we may well regard with distrust." James Garner, in his textbook of political science, took the same position. State activity could not be regulated by general rules but had to be adjusted to correspond to the special conditions under which it occurred. Westel Willoughby maintained that from "the nature of the case, there are no precise limits that can be placed to the extent to which a popularly organized government may go in the diminution of individual freedom." What the state could and could not do was to be resolved solely by expediency. The definition of its scope lay within the domain of politics, not political theory. In each particular case, a judgment would have to be made whether public control was more advantageous than disadvantageous. Thus, the "only point here insisted upon is that there is no *a priori* or fixed limit which can be placed to governmental activity, but that the assumption of each function must rest upon its own utilitarian basis." Finally, Lester Ward voiced the opinion that no universally valid standards existed by which one could determine legislation. It was obvious that "each special issue must be considered upon its own merits. Its advisability will depend upon its own special nature and upon the circumstances under which it must operate."[31]

Paradoxically, then, a major result of the retreat from politics engaged in by reformers (in contrast to that of the Transcendentalists) was not that the state was confined within strict boundaries or that it was cast aside as unessential. It turned out to be a highly useful instrument by which society, released from the straitjacket of natural law, could promote its own welfare. Because the social interest, now concretized in terms of a variable experience divorced from theory, was supreme, there could be no limitations on the means by which it was furthered. Admittedly, most of the reformers did not insist dogmatically on governmental intervention as an end in itself or glorify the state; yet they did believe that in principle no barriers could be set up to circumscribe the power of government. Even a pervasive regulation of industry, if experience dictated its necessity, could not be flatly dismissed. And, in fact, throughout this period, "problems" continually arose that demanded political action, precedents were established by which further encroachments upon the marketplace were rationalized, and social forces found that the state could greatly maximize their welfare through a reallocation of property. Still, if such intervention was to be vindicated and depicted as consonant with the American tradition, the obliteration of one important distinction was required. It was imperative that liberty be construed as something other than freedom from physical coercion.

CHAPTER VII

THE NEW FREEDOM

Republicans had perceived force as consisting in the application of physical constraints upon the person or in the deprivation of property. Private relationships, so long as they were voluntary, were not regarded as subversive of freedom. The central task of the state was thought to reside in the protection of the citizen's person and possessions from the use of force. The creation of the polity did not mean that natural rights had been yielded, for only the right to self-defense, and all that it implied, had been delegated to the government. Although republicans conceded the necessity for the state, they did not deny its coercive aspects. Indeed, they were concerned about obtaining the consent of the ruled precisely because they realized that law was, by its very nature, compulsive. It could not be justly imposed, therefore, without the individual's approval, either tacit or otherwise. Because the state, and the state alone, had the power of making laws, that is, of applying force "legitimately," it was important to circumscribe it within a well-defined sphere. Institutional arrangements, such as checks and balances, and an explicit enumeration, through a written constitution, of the common objects for which government had been established were necessary to ensure that coercion would not be applied "arbitrarily." But whether it was employed capriciously or not, the fact remains that government constituted a monopoly on the legitimate use of force. Its commands could not be disobeyed without incurring confinement, loss of life, or dispossession of property.

Democratic collectivists departed from this conception of republican individualism by equating social (or economic) to political power. Force was now perceived to exist, in various degrees, in a multitude of purely voluntary relationships. Reformers admitted that such compulsion was less tangible; yet, they claimed that social and economic "pressures" though less obvious, were no less real in their effects. The main problem facing the analyst was to discover where such pressures existed. Once this had been achieved, the remaining difficulty was to bring about their reduction or elimination. If nonpolitical agencies did not prove efficacious in this regard, the state could be called upon to expand freedom by acting "positively" to release the individual from such social bonds.

Such an outlook, in essence, meant that the coercive characteristics of the state were not to be acknowledged. It entailed no contradiction to assert that men could be forced to be free. This line of thinking stemmed directly from the central tenets of empirical collectivism. Because the polity was only a branch of society, there could be no difference in kind between actions undertaken by the state and those performed by private individuals or groups. Both were forms of social activity. Government was only an accumulation of those instances in which society had chosen a specifically political mechanism to obtain its ends. It was nonsensical to search for liberty in a static relation. Again, the pragmatic element was present. Freedom, if it had any concrete meaning at all, could pertain only to a socially preferred result, not to any abstract quality.

This transition from "free government" to "free society" meant that what republicans had ascribed only to the coercive aspects of the state could now be predicated of the behavior of individuals dealing freely with each other. Again, key concepts were yanked out of the political context in which they had arisen and were given content in social terms. As previously seen, corporations were often indicted for autocratic rule; some writers even went so far as to attribute sovereignty to them and, indeed, to an array of private organizations. In addition, the trusts were accused of destroying property through unbridled competition, as surely as if they had done so by an overt use of physical force. Taxation, reformers also claimed, was being exercised by private individuals. And monopoly, hitherto regarded as the granting by government of a legally exclusive privilege to engage in commerce, retained its sinister connotation, yet was now held to apply to companies that had obtained a large, if undefined, share of the market. Perhaps the greatest change of all occurred in the meaning of the term "equality". For republicans, it had denoted an identity of rights or simple equality before the law. Progressives, attacking what they considered to be moral egoism, now socialized it by identifying it with a more "equitable" distribution of wealth and other valued attributes. Indeed, this conception of equality often functioned as the criterion by which results were adjudged. The uneven possession of wealth was seen as a threat to the autonomy of the individual. Freedom, then, inhered in the elimination of disparities, particularly those economic in character, not physical constraints.

Reformers began their attack on the static notion of liberty by portraying free government as a system in which freedom had been snuffed out by a selfish few. In accordance with the leitmotiv of changing conditions, they insisted that a change in the social structure, without any corresponding alteration in the political system, could result in a change in the practical meaning of a concept. Such was the case with limited government. Industrial evolution had rendered the traditional notion of freedom obsolete. "The actual liberty of the individual may vary greatly without any change in the legal or constitutional organization of society. A political system essentially undemocratic would be much less destructive of individual liberty in a society where the economic life was simple and ownership widely diffused than in a community possessing a wealthy capitalist class on the one hand and an army of wage-earners on the other."[1] They likewise asserted that in certain instances the principle of voluntary contract had produced outcomes exactly the reverse "of that which the conception originally contemplated." A rigid adherence to its sanctity had "given rise to rules and decisions which, tested by their practical operation," defeated liberty.[2] Some progressives even discovered that the greater range of choices offered by an expanding industrial economy made for slavery, not liberation. Thus, in *The Promise of American Life* (1909), described by Theodore Roosevelt as a "most profound and illuminating study of our national conditions," Herbert Croly wrote that "it would be far more true to say that the popular enjoyment of practically unrestricted economic opportunities is precisely the condition which makes for individual bondage."[3]

To rectify this situation, proponents of democratic collectivism persistently emphasized that the force of society had to be brought to bear where conditions were subversive of the actual freedom of the citizens. Now, progressives did not deify the state or adopt an explicitly Hegelian stance to the effect that freedom could come only through government. They believed that social forces could often create liberty through organs other than government, for "democracy makes use of all existing agencies for the attainment of its industrial program."[4] Yet, if voluntary methods could not bring about the desired result, then the state, as a social tool, could be called upon to expand the realm of free action. Thus, Lester Ward alleged that it was the task of society, employing the state apparatus if necessary, to keep open the avenues of liberty and that old notions of personal autonomy were outmoded in the light of the fact that competition had produced combination; "the paradox therefore is that *individual freedom can only come through social regulation.*" Henry Demarest Lloyd vociferated that freedom resided in the submission to the will of all, not in the egoistic pursuit of wealth. "We can become individual only by submitting to be bound to others. We extend our freedom only by finding new laws to obey . . . The more relations, ties, duties, the more 'individual.' " Woodrow Wilson similarly maintained that despotism could be eradicated by the expansion of the power of the state. He espoused what he called the "new freedom," noting that liberty consisted in "something more than being let alone. The program of a government of freedom must in these days be positive, not negative merely." Wilson observed that tyranny had learned how to "wear the mere guise of industry," and, practically quoting Rousseau, demanded that men be interfered with in order to set them free, protesting that the individual was caught in a "great confused nexus."[5] Other reformers expressed the same beliefs in a variety of ways. At the root of all their statements was the concept that liberty was not "absence of restraint but presence of order . . . agreeable to the prevailing sense of right whatever that may be."[6] Hence, pertaining to freedom, no substantive distinctions could be made between decisions enforced by law and those arrived at by other means. In the eyes of reformers, government became "simply a collection of cases in which society in its corporate capacity has assumed to control certain operations"[7] Political power, therefore, could be meaningfully employed as some kind of "countervailing" force to industrial "power," the public and the private sectors being put in a proper "balance."[8] The application of law could emancipate the individual from social bondage.

It was on the basis of this complex of assumptions that the trusts, at least initially, were held largely responsible for the tyranny that was enmeshing the American people. They already had been denounced as detrimental to the existence of competition and undemocratic. Possibly anticipating the rejoinders that the existence of inefficient competitors was not to the public advantage and that business was best managed "undemocratically," progressives berated concentration (and what had made it possible) as precisely equivalent to the exercise of naked, destructive force, as going well beyond simple rule without consent. Because it undermined in the most fundamental way the position of those who had steadfastly opposed reform on the ground that government was designed solely to prevent aggression, this contention appeared to be all the more damaging and therefore found ubiquitous and labored expression in the literature.

Concerning the alleged abuses of industrial power, the starting point of the argument was the assertion that governments had often given companies the exclusive privilege to manufacture products or to engage in trade in a certain geographical area; this was a legal prohibition, physically preventing competitors from contesting with the favorites of the political authority. But progressives pragmatically postulated that if the same situation obtained from the apparently free interplay of individuals on the market, then in practice the companies which had achieved such a "privileged" position were exercising just as much force as those which had been legally insulated from competition. Clothed in the "mere guise of industry," as Wilson had said, this coercion, although economic in character, was no less invidious in its effects. Consequently, any legalistic definition of monopoly was rejected out of hand. Henry Lloyd admonished that it excluded the "whole body of facts which people include in their definition," dismissing "a great public question by a mere play on words." Likening the struggle against "monopoly" in nineteenth-century America to that against government-enforced monopoly in seventeenth-century England, Lloyd declared that violence could not only be physical but economic as well. "It makes no practical difference to the people whether the reason they are not free to go into the tobacco business is because an exclusive privilege has been granted by a queen to her favorite, or because it has been won by a group of capitalists using rapid-fire bank accounts in a market war as batteries to destroy competitors and compel the community to pay perpetual indemnity." Citing a report of Congress that the price of coal was one dollar a ton more than the fair competitive market price, Lloyd asseverated that because coal was a "necessity" and a large part of its production was controlled by a small group of men, the consumer was being literally forced to buy at the price set by the trust. "You pay it under compulsion; you must have the coal; you are not allowed to buy of any one but the members of the combination; you are given no choice as to the price."[9]

Economists Henry C. Adams and Edmund James similarly censured unregulated monopoly as resulting in the accumulation of arbitrary power. Adams related that in the past it had sprung from royal grants or charters; now it arose from industrial activity itself. James alluded to the bonds drawn tight by private enterprise in certain cases and declared that the intervention of government would be necessary if the individual were to be set free. "[Adam] Smith called upon private enterprise to check and circumscribe government activity; we are forced to call upon government to circumscribe and regulate private enterprise." Animated by a kindred spirit, Woodrow Wilson inaugurated his policy of governmental interference with the operation of the market by stating that it would free enterprise from its chains. "Our purpose is the restoration of freedom. We propose to prevent private property by law, to see to it that the methods by which monopolies have been built up are legally made impossible. We design that the limitations on private enterprise shall be removed."[10] In short, there was general agreement that the "monopoly" which had arisen on the free market was completely comparable to that which had been mandated by the state in previous eras.[11]

The notion that coercion could reside in something other than the erection of physical obstacles led not only to the redefinition of monopoly in social terms. The identification of the power of government with that of industry sparked a similar and far-flung transformation of other concepts, culminating in analyses and commentaries which, in seemingly endless ways, blurred the distinction between compulsion and freedom. Richard Ely, for instance, revealed that the only significant difference between big business and government was that the former was far more dangerous to freedom that the latter. "Vast corporations are a menace to liberty. They interfere with free thought and free speech and a free vote ten times where government does so once. "Another critic, William J. Ghent, assailed free production and exchange by likening it to the system that it had succeeded. In America a new "feudalism" had arisen, one which obligated those who wished to survive to make their "peace" with those who had the "disposition of the livings." This feudalism was different in form from that of Edward I "yet based upon the same status of lord, agent, and underling." Lester Ward proposed his scheme of attractive legislation in which the government would create opportunities and foster action along lines conducive to the public good. Implicitly denying the compulsion inherent in the taxing power, he conveyed the belief that attractive legislation, such as the tariff and subsidies, rested on rewards and not punishments. Herbert Croly, whose predilection was to accept the vital assumptions of other reformers and then expound them in a manner congenial to his nationalistic proclivities, constantly equated political to economic power and, to complicate matters, insisted that Jefferson had also. Depicting power as "usually derived from the association of a number of individuals for a common purpose," he deplored the Jeffersonian fear of its concentration. Its growth, Croly hypothesized, would further the interests of the community and would not endanger freedom if democratically supervised; hence, public regulation of business was essential to keeping force within reasonable bounds.[12]

Certain theorists even went beyond the presumption that undemocratic and coercive elements were simply present in the economy and deduced that voluntary organizations could be treated as full-scale governments. This line of reasoning was most conspicuously, though not exclusively, adopted by Arthur Bentley. He did not give a rigorous, unambiguous definition of politics, deeming it as inhering only in the balancing of interests. Although admitting the belief that physical force lay at the base of law partook of a certain measure of truth, he posited the existence of other "pressures" which were not violent, so that physical force was only one among many "forms of social technique." Appraising a concept by its effects, he concluded that a corporation was essentially a government. Certain technical methods, such as hanging, used by a government were not indulged in by corporations, but this difference was a mere matter of detail. Besides, corporations often put people to death by "carelessness or by parsimony." "A corporation is a government through and through. It is itself a balancing of interests, even though it presents itself in many of its activities as a unit. It has been forced into corporate form by the struggling of the interests upon one another . . . Possibly there are as many forms of corporate government as there are of political government, and possibly those corporate government forms can ultimately be classified on the very lines used for the classification of political governments." Bentley also remarked that a labor union could be considered a government. In any case, the portrayal of a corporation as a political unit was another manifestation of the tendency to obfuscate the differences between private and public action.[13]

One important derivative of the attribution of sovereignty, or at least "partial" sovereignty, to corporations and to business in general was the misconception that prices and wages were not determined by the bargaining of sellers and buyers but set by the entrepreneur. Consequently, it was argued, some manufacturers were really taxing the people, and at a scandalous rate at that. The concept of taxation, hitherto restricted to the state's confiscation of income, was thus extended to agreements freely arrived at in the market. A price regarded as too high or a wage as too low was actually a surreptitious means by which the cunning capitalist diverted social gains into his pockets. Lester Ward submitted that private enterprise taxed the consumer, remonstrating that for many commodities the people paid two or three times as much as would cover cost and "exchange at fair wages and fair profits." Referring to monopoly prices (which he did not define), Ward observed that no "government in the world has now, or ever had, the power to enforce such an extortion as this. It is a governing power in the interest of favored individuals, which exceeds that of the most powerful monarch or despot that ever wielded a scepter." Similarly, Brooks Adams called attention to the transportation tax levied by the railroads and charged that other monopolies also had usurped the power of taxation. He saw it as self-evident that because one company or a small group of companies "controlled" production of necessities, the consumer was being victimized and the monopoly in question was exacting tribute from the populace. "Nor could they well have done so [endured monopoly] without constraint by overpowering physical force, for the possession of a monopoly of a necessary of life by an individual, or by a small privileged class, is tantamount to investing a minority, contemptible alike in numbers and in physical force, with an arbitrary and unlimited power to tax the majority, not for public, but for private purposes." Finally, John Bates Clark, representative of the more conservative wing of the collectivist movement, avowed that the high prices imposed by corporations were a form of taxation.[14]

Another consequence of the view that force could be economic in nature was that the term "collectivism" was attached in industrial developments which had transpired within the framework of private enterprise. The status of property had changed radically under the regime of free contract. It no longer signified what it once had. Collective control of material goods had replaced individual ownership. Some theorists greeted this change favorably. Charles W. Eliot, for example, related that while socialism was hostile to property, collectivism was not. He explained that the widespread diffusion of corporate stocks and bonds provided an excellent illustration of collectivism strengthening democracy and resisting socialism by devising "safe but mobile forms of property." Here again was the idea pressed by Croly and others. Association as such was collectivist and constituted power. There was no difference in kind between political and voluntary association, for both involved cooperation for a common purpose. A variation on this theme, with somewhat different conclusions, was the belief that the trusts were putting an end to private property, something which many progressives welcomed. Thus, Walter Lippmann, always concrete-bound in his orientation, exclaimed that since, in contrast to the farmer, the modern shareholder did not see what he owned, private property was perishing under modern capitalism. Although it remained in agricultural land and "competitive" business, the trusts were steadily diminishing its sphere. It is surprising yet true that the "trust movement is doing what no conspirator or revolutionist could ever do: It is sucking the life out of private property . . . You cannot conduct the great industries and preserve intact the principles of private property. And so the trusts are organizing private property out of existence, are altering its nature so radically that very little remains but the title and the ancient theory."[15]

Evaluating matters from a pragmatic perspective, the critics of free government also suggested that property was being both destroyed and confiscated by the trusts. Not only were they taxing citizens by means of high prices and low wages; businessmen were also depriving others of property by the very nature of their competitive practices. An action, if it had an undesirable result which could have been produced by physical force, implied the exercise of some kind of coercion. If a man had his property stolen, the value of his material goods was decreased. If a "predatory" practice had the end result of decreasing the worth of his property, although no physical force was utilized, the effect was the same as if coercion had been used. The only difference was that the application of economic force was more subtle. Hence, case after case was cited in which repugnant practices had lowered the value of someone's property. For instance, Lloyd expostulated that the railroads used force against mineowners by setting transportation rates so high that they were selling their products at a loss, with the intention of inducing them to sell out. Property, in his view, could be used in such a way as to make a mockery of freedom, by forcing others to submit to an agreement they found undesirable or face an unpleasant alternative. Edmund James asserted, reasoning in like manner, that if the outcome of certain industrial policies was to lower the value of property, then coercion had been utilized. Indeed, "if a railroad makes a discrimination in its charges as between citizens, it destroys the value of property just as certainly as if it took a force of men and marched to the place and destroyed one of the buildings belonging to one party."[16]

At this juncture, the clarifying point should be most strongly made that, even if one were to make the dubious concession of granting the accuracy of the cited and usually unsupported indictments of relatively uninhibited enterprise, it would not in the least follow that redefinitions were in order. All that would be demonstrated is that, under given circumstances, freedom produced outcomes which many might consider undesirable. Whatever the impact for political theory of such results, the power of the market is not to be blithely identified with outright physical force. Even in the extreme case of only one producer of a commodity, consumers who feel imposed upon have the choice of shifting expenditures to similar (or not so similar) items or of patronizing new competitors in the field. As long as entry into an industry or trade is not barred by law, monopoly, in the sense of a business immune to market forces and consumer preferences, cannot exist. The situation is entirely different when we are dealing with governmental edicts. When the state declares, for instance, that a given company, or group of companies for that matter, alone may provide an article, there exists no possibility of free choice, for those who attempt to compete will be forcibly excluded from so doing. Liberty pertains only to the removal of physical impediments and is, in that sense, a "negative" conception. For like reasons, it is fallacious to identify voluntary organizations with government (in whole or in part), to assail certain market prices as equivalent to taxation, or to affirm that property is assaulted by changing market evaluations of goods or the existence of corporate, as distinct from individual, ownership. The intellectual and linguistic muddle surrounding all of these concepts was the inevitable result of attempting to retain the esteemed traditional terminology while infusing it with a novel content, of putting the new wine of progressivism into the old, venerable bottles of revolutionary republicanism.

The same arguments used to prove that business was tyrannical could be applied to industrial activity of whatever scale, indeed even to noneconomic phenomena. Force was perceived, and in reformist logic existed, wherever human decision did not correspond to the theorist's vision of the good. Large corporations, small companies, and business in general were discovered to be using force to some degree. Pressures were detected in a variety of other areas as well. In each case, it was shown how conditions were unsatisfactory from a humane viewpoint and how the state was obliged to intervene to secure freedom by altering the "facts." Each reformer projected his own values into his definition of freedom, choosing what situation he was to analyze, what needs were to be regarded as "true," and to what extent and in what manner these needs were to be satisfied. The "solution" to the "problem" was presented as a restoration of freedom.

For example, Roscoe Pound reprobated a court decision to the effect that the prices of a company store could not be regulated by the government, objecting that "there may be a compulsion in fact where there is none in law." Thorstein Veblen bemoaned the unfortunate course of industry since its emancipation from guild regulations. Capitalist control of industry made the worker dependent upon the will of the employer; he could not work as he chose or dispose of his product in the manner he desired. The conditions upon which his existence depended were not set by him. Free contract was a sham in many instances, because the employer could rely on economic force to compel the worker to accept his offer on his own terms.

Under the current *de facto* standardization of economic life enforced by the machine industry, it may frequently happen that an individual or a group, *e.g.*, of workmen, has not a *de facto* power of free contract. A given workman's livelihood can perhaps, practically, be found only on acceptance of one specific contract offered, perhaps not at all. But the coercion which in this way bears upon his choice through the standardization of industrial procedure is neither assault and battery nor breach of contract, and it is, therefore, not repugnant to the principles of natural liberty. Through controlling the processes of industry in which alone, practically, given workmen can find their livelihood, the owners of these processes may bring pecuniary pressure to bear upon the choice of the workmen.

Similarly, Walter Weyl, who earnestly urged that "dying young should be forbidden by law," reproved the compulsion exerted by employers on their workers and exhorted the state to extend the freedom of employees by interfering with the terms of the labor contract. In an industrial economy "the chief restrictions upon liberty are economic, not legal, and the chief prerogatives desired are economic, not political . . . A law forbidding a woman to work in the textile mills at night is a law increasing rather than restricting *her* liberty, simply because it takes from the employer *his* former right to compel her through sheer economic pressure to work at night when she would prefer to work by day."[17]

All in all, then, progressives found that coercion extended across a great range of phenomena under a regime of free contract. Specifically, what the critic of constitutional government singled out as a use of force depended on what he held dear. And values varied widely among reformers. Still, there existed a marked propensity to equate the "good," and thus liberty, to self-sacrifice for the "community as a whole." The general ethical standard by which the proponents of "positive democracy" ferreted out and analyzed problems, that "presence of order agreeable to the prevailing sense of right," was altruism. Taking cognizance of the decisions made in the marketplace and elsewhere, they noted that people in many cases chose to spend their money, not to alleviate the suffering of others or to raise the standard of living of those economically worse off, but to indulge their personal desires. This situation was seen as a fundamental defect of free government.

Republicans admittedly did not evolve a fully elaborated ethical theory; but, in so far as they used the term "selfish" in a pejorative sense, it was to refer to a state of affairs in which a partial interest was satisfying itself at the expense of other interests through a forcible transfer of wealth. The right to property meant only that the wealth an individual acquired by noncoercive means was his to dispose of as he saw fit. Under a system of constitutional government, a man was free to spend his income solely on personal consumption or, if he so desired, entirely on helping those less prosperous, or some mixture of the two. The choice was his, and his alone, to make. Correspondingly, free government was not sapped by an individual's decision to devote himself to "social service" or even to live in a commune (as some Transcendentalists had done). As long as association remained voluntary, no man's liberty was in danger.

The deification of self-sacrifice proved to be inimical to republican individualism for several reasons. In the first place, it was fully reflective of, and conversely served to strengthen, the prejudice that individuals were cogs in the large whole, which could survive and function harmoniously only if the "parts" renounced their metaphysical and moral independence, abandoned the pursuit of special aims, and embraced cooperation, thereby toiling for society's benefit alone. Additionally, the crusade against egoism, along with the personification of the community, helped drive out any zetetic consideration of what a man had or had not earned, even within the framework of the social organism, for the accent was on the sharing of wealth, not its creation. Lastly, it resulted in the importunity that men be forced to act altruistically. Again, collectivists did not perceive the state as the only vehicle by which men could be made to promote the public welfare. They clearly deemed social persuasion to be a valuable tool. Still, it was held that if all else failed, state action could be properly invoked to mitigate the effects of egoism.

In this context, the persistent demand that ethics be applied to the organization of society becomes understandable. "Any economic proposition which cannot be stated in ethical terms is false."[18] Practically every collectivist tract, whatever its subject nature, made some reference to the desirability of altruistic action. From the literature of this period can be gleaned innumerable paeans to the ethics of social service. The central goal of reformers was to inculcate the social spirit by undermining the notion of individual independence. Once this end had been accomplished, the concrete injunction to act so as to benefit the community would be more readily accepted. "It [moral individualism] has its roots in the notion that the consciousness of each person is wholly private, a self-inclosed continent, intrinsically independent of the ideas, wishes, purposes of everybody else. But when men act, they act in a common and public world. This is the problem to which the theory isolated and independent conscious minds gave rise: Given feelings, ideas, desires, which have nothing to do with one another, how can actions proceeding from them be controlled in a social or public interest? Given an egoistic consciousness, how can action which has regard for others take place?"[19] In great part, this subversion of the integrity of the individual's consciousness was attained through the positing of a social self. The reification of society made each mind a product of social forces lying outside the individual. In any case, the thrust was on the communalizing of ethics. "The new spirit," exulted Walter Weyl, "is social. Its base is broad. It involves common action and a common lot. It emphasizes social rather than private ethics, social rather than individual responsiblity."[20]

Clergymen were in the forefront of those depreciating capitalism as a selfish system satisfying the needs of an avaricious few. Ignoring what had been considered as the central preoccupation of Christianity, namely, the concern for the purity of the individual soul, advocates of the Social Gospel shifted the emphasis of Christianity to social salvation.[21] Although most of them wanted voluntary action, they were not averse to calling upon the state to promote "social justice." Lyman Abbott rejected communism yet decided that Christ's teachings held that property was a trust to be used for the benefit of all. Washington Gladden lambasted the wage system in so far as it was based on competition only; Christian ethics would inject the altruistic element into an egoistic society. Walter Rauschenbusch saw Jesus as favoring the oppressed and exploited, and he denounced the selfishness of individualism.[22] Other servants of God were equally critical of the limited state, although only a few advocated a communal division of property.[23] Even those who were not directly part of the Social Gospel movement interpreted Christianity as a moral justification for other-directed action. Thus, William D. P. Bliss claimed that the one great motive which had produced both socialism and social reform was altruism, which sprang originally from the Christian faith. Henry Lloyd and Edward Bellamy also alluded to the precepts of Christ in supporting their views.[24]

Criticism of free government for the selfishness it spawned was made in more secular terms as well. Westel Willoughby maintained that the highest good for man was a social one and that man realized his potential only when he sought his good in the good of others and of society at large, vouchsafing that his will would thereby be "purified from selfishness." With increasing civilization would come "higher morality, broadened altruism, and widened intellectual horizon." Prominent novelist William Dean Howells condemned America as a country lacking kindness, one where every man was for himself. Woodrow Wilson decried the competitive system as magnifying self-interest and thrusting out love and compassion, stating that "certainly modern individualism has much about it that is hateful, too hateful to last." Edward Bellamy exalted self-sacrifice in his works, objecting that under "negative democracy," the people were more concerned with their personal stakes than the general welfare. In an early notebook he commented that the true "Religion of Solidarity requires in all cases the fulfillment of the instinct of the whole, obedience to that universal which may indifferently coincide with the assertion or abrogation of my individuality." Herbert Croly shunned Jeffersonianism as "tantamount in practice to a species of vigorous, licensed, and purified selfishness," disparaging it for making the responsibilities of government "negative" and those of the individual "positive." He insisted that American democracy ideally was grounded in the assumption that every man should serve his fellow men. "In the complete democracy a man must in some way be made to serve the nation in the very act of contributing to his own individual fulfillment. Not until his personal action is dictated by disinterested motives can there by any such harmony between private and public interests. To ask an individual citizen continually to sacrifice his recognized private interest to the welfare of his countrymen is to make an impossible demand, and yet just such a continual sacrifice is apparently required of an individual in a democratic state." Henry Demarest Lloyd declared vehemently that industry was a "fight of every man for himself . . . the main doctrine of industry since Adam Smith has been the fallacy that the self-interest of the individual was a sufficient guide to the welfare of the individual and society." He implored that the interests of all constitute the rule of all, the strong serve the weak, and the first be the last. Finally, Lester Ward celebrated altruism as "far higher and nobler" than egoism, entreating "society as a whole" to reap the benefits generated by the activities of the "elite of mankind."[25]

The younger economists, many of them trained in Germany,[26] came to the conclusion that self-interest should not be regarded as the only factor operative in economic life and that orthodox theory cast out altruistic elements as an abnormal factor. The presumption that men always knew their interests was false, they thought.[27] Selfishness was not an adequate guide to material-oriented action. Richard Ely, fully representative in this respect, contended that egoism and altruism were incompatible and that God had to triumph over Mammon. The new economics would summon forth the state to correct deficiencies, preventing the "greedy and the avaricious" from "grinding the poor" under the slogans of laissez-faire and free competition and affirming the principle of self-sacrifice. John Bates Clark suggested that the notion of "economic man" was false, contrary to human nature, and that all ideal wants were unselfish. Men, he felt, ought to be altruistic, whereas society should act egoistically. He postulated that the "universal interdependence of parts is a primary characteristic of social organisms; each member exists and labors, not for himself, but for the whole, and is dependent on the whole for remuneration."[28] Other reform economists echoed the views of Ely and Clark.

Occasionally, the thought was ventilated that perhaps egoism and altruism were not fully antithetical, that they could be joined into some sort of higher unity, or even that altruism was not fully desirable. However, it was still propagated that men had to live for the community. Thus, Dewey related that altruism may be evil, but his objections, for the most part, reduced to affirming that in certain situations it led to egoism, in ourselves and others! Indeed, the professedly individualistic side of his moral criterion for institutions was indubitably collectivist. "The test is whether a given custom or law sets free individual capacities in such a way as to make them available for the development of the general happiness or the common good."[29]

The moral presumptions of progressives, while (rather interestingly) seldom brought to bear in narrow treatment of the "facts," did lead directly to the reformulation of the concepts of liberty and equality. Because society is no more than the men who comprise it, the doctrine that the individual had to sacrifice himself for the community turned out to mean, and could only mean, that some had to labor for the benefit of others. Inevitably, the interpretation of altruism was that those better off (in whatever respect) than their fellow men had to act so as to aid those less well endowed. It was now possible to give an entirely new meaning to the concept of equality, while still retaining the label itself. For republicans, it was purely political in its significance, designating nothing more than an identity of rights or an equality before the law. Reformers, however, drained it of its political meaning, charging, in the words of Herbert Croly, that in practice the system of equal rights had "proved to be inimical to individual liberty, efficiency, and distinction."[30] True equality was found to inhere in the elimination of social and economic differences. And such equality was gratuitously identified with freedom. In no respect had the change from an explicitly political to a social perspective been so consummate.

The predilection, tacit or otherwise, of many theorists was to associate the good, altruistically defined, to liberation and simply leave it at that. Others, not content with so doing, followed a seemingly less subjective approach, yet one confirming in full the equalitarian biases of the former group. The argument began with the assumption, one deriving verisimilitude, at least in part, from the altruistic morality, that liberty was to be linked to the fulfillment of needs. Lester Ward, for example, avowed that it resided in the power to act according to one's desires. Herbert Croly believed that the crucial condition of freedom was the development of the highest possible standard of living. Edward Ross took the same tack when he stated that there was no sociological differences between public and private action. The only question to be considered was whether the state or the individual could perform the task more efficiently. Such tasks were conceived to be the satisfaction of human desires. And Richard Ely, recounting that socialists were right in saying that the chief restrictions on freedom were pecuniary in character, drew the logical conclusion from the premises most progressives accepted when he identified the failure to satisfy a need, for whatever reason, with compulsion. The result, he pragmatically claimed, was the same as would be engendered by a law prohibiting its realization. A case in point is that of a poor man who "wishes to spend the winter in Egypt because he has consumption. No statute stands in the way, and yet he is as unable to go as he would be if prohibited by ten thousand legislative enactments. But this is not all. Restrictions proceed from lack of economic resources, and compulsion is connected with our economic necessities."[31] On the basis of these and like suppositions, rather disconcerting admonishments that "absolute" freedom is a "myth"[32] and "all things are now and always have been governed by force,"[33] often made surprisingly by the same writers who heralded in society an awesome power for emancipation, are fully understandable. Because no man, or collection of men, possesses limitless capital and knowledge, humanity can never escape some degree of slavery; nature itself must be seen as exploitative.

More importantly, in so far as the practical aims of progressives are concerned, it is not only reality which hobbles man. It is also obviously the case that if freedom is equated to the power to act, the existence of socioeconomic inequality implies its uneven distribution. In pragmatic terms, the "inordinate" possession of values of whatever sort by some becomes an obstacle to the gratification of the needs of others, because if they were distributed more equally, the result would be that more people would have more of their demands granted. Progressives seldom expressly addressed the possible, and cogent, objections that those whose resources were redistributed would then have less of their wants fulfilled and that the sum total of liberty could not therefore be augmented. The period's intoxication with equality prevented a sober treatment of these issues. The underlying and generally unarticulated sentiment was that interpersonal comparisons of utility were possible and that the needs of those who had incomes less than the norm were truer and more urgent than those who had incomes above it. Equality constituted some sort of equilibrium point, the burden falling on the critic to justify departures from it.

The elimination of physical force, therefore, was not a means to attaining liberty. In fact, its use was imperative, in some cases, if economic force was to be done away with. "The freedom of an agent who is merely released from direct external obstructions is formal and empty," as Dewey said.[34] Actual freedom signified the actual enjoyment of something. Wherever some people were more satisfied than others, conditions had to be altered. Distrust even extended to those differentials in personal qualities which brought about such discrepancies. Thus, those who posited inequalities in mental ability as sanctioning corresponding inequalities in wealth earned the opprobrium of Lester Ward, always sensitive to such arguments, who likened the use of intelligence, admittedly of the merely cunning variety, to the application of brute force. "Thus the claim that the superior intelligence of certain members of society justifies the social inequalities that make up most of the misery of the world does not differ in any respect from the claim of the physically strongest men in a barbaric race to seize and possess the handsomest women and the finest oxen." Indeed, some empirical collectivists did not regard only material differences as violative of freedom. They also saw, and quite truly given their premises, disparities of other generally valued qualities as nefarious. In this vein, John Dewey propounded that the "individualistic formula tends in practice to emphasize the freedom of the man who has the power at the expense of his neighbor weaker in health, in intellectual ability, in worldly goods, and in social influence."[35]

The greatest stress, however, was laid on the injustice of

economic inequality. Practically all reformers, either implicitly or explicity, damned differences in wealth as, ipso facto, destructive of liberty. The minimization of such differences, however obtained, would increase the aggregate freedom of the community. The critique of Edward Bellamy was entirely illustrative in this respect, if carried to conclusions few were willing to adopt. Intimately associating freedom and want satisfaction, Bellamy denounced economic disparities as a form of coercion. He reasoned that whoever owned something which someone else needed to live was a slavedriver. Those without capital, harried by hunger and other needs, were forced to work for those who had it. In fact, the putatively free worker was a more degraded figure than the chattel slave, who at least acknowledged the reality of his status. The capitalist system presented a complex series of relationships in which men were dependent on each other for their very living. Freedom, Bellamy cried, could not exist when mere individuals controlled socially valuable goods. "You overlooked the plain fact that anybody who by any means, however indirect or remote, took away or curtailed one's means of subsistence attacked his life quite as dangerously as it could be done with knife or bullet." The general welfare necessitated that the common ownership of property be instituted and society, through the state, guarantee work and absolutely equal incomes to all citizens, so that property could not be wielded as a weapon. Liberty mandated that the principle of military service be applied to labor on a universal scale, leaving those who refused to work for the nation without any means of support.[36]

Many other proponents of the "positive state," if by no means all, also excoriated economic inequality as tyrannical, but they somehow managed to avoid the conclusion that a categorically equal division of property was necessary. They simply stipulated that wealth be transferred from those with higher to those with lower incomes by a variety of measures, such as industrial regulation and taxation. In this way, more valid needs would be gratified and the total freedom of the community maximized. Concentrating their attention on specific problems, they always envisaged a contrasting and more desirable situation, one by which present reality was assessed. In each case, they showed that if the facts were altered by the state or other agencies, the range of desires satisfied would be greater. If the worker had more wealth and the employer less, bargaining would be more equal and wages higher. Similarly, if more competition prevailed in a certain line of production, prices would be lower. If scabs were prevented from crossing the picket line, the strike would succeed and thereby benefit the workers. If, in general, prices were lower, profits reduced, and wages higher, then the people as a whole would have more of their needs fulfilled. Thus, concrete freedom, the only idea of freedom that really mattered, took into account the desires of individuals and strove to adjust them in a more egalitariam synthesis, so that the area of liberty was expanded as much as possible. Abstract freedom, on the contrary, was in practice antagonistic to man's autonomy. It blithely permitted actions that would diminish the level of satisfaction of some men for the welfare of others. Hence, Dewey brought out that the entry of additional workers into a given labor market might reduce the wages paid to other workers, thereby violating their freedom, and he deplored competition of this kind. "The maximum freedom of one individual consistent with equal *concrete* or *total* freedom of others, would indeed represent a high moral ideal. But the individualistic formula is condemned by the fact that it has in mind only an abstract, mechanical, external, and hence formal freedom."[37]

Therefore, in the name of both equality and freedom, neither now construed in a political sense, critics of free government urged that material gaps be narrowed. Indeed, of all progressive demands, greater equality of possessions was the most ubiquitous. Clergyman Lyman Abbott discovered that the concentration of wealth was America's greatest peril and that a more equable distribution was needed. "The main benefit enjoyed by the railroad king who owns two hundred million dollars," he trumpeted, "is the right to administer a great property for the benefit of the common people." Washington Gladden propounded that workmen ought to have a larger share of the national wealth and that the possessor of wealth was under the responsibility to help the less fortunate. Walter Lippmann pleaded for a better distribution of wealth and decreed that the working class had an excellent use for any additional money it might secure. Economist Simon Patten, an intellectual progenitor of those who in a later period postulated an affluent society, averred that before the nineteenth century only pain or "deficit" economies obtained; but now there had finally come about a social surplus, one which had to be devoted to the promotion of the common good and distributed more equitably. In like fashion, Herbert Croly, castigating the wage system for creating a class of "essential economic dependents," flayed the existing allocation of material benefits as an "inevitable outcome of the chaotic individualism of our political and economic organization." Calling for a tax on corporations according to their percentage of profit, he avowed that in "becoming responsible for the subordination of the individual to the demand of a dominant and constructive national purpose, the American state will in effect be making itself responsible for a morally and socially desirable distribution of wealth." Lastly, Walter Weyl declaimed against great fortunes, appealing for a "reasonable and just distribution of the product of industry, a fair adjustment as between wages, profits, interest, rent, and the share of the state." Taxation of some for the welfare of others was objurgated by individualists, he wrote, but in the socialized democracy, a more equal distribution of wealth would be openly sought.[38]

In summation, the firm denial of the differences between public and private actions, the central premise of the acerbic critique of "static" liberty, was by no means a conclusion arrived at haphazardly. Rather, it was a logical development within the posited theoretical, or antitheoretical, framework. It followed necessarily from the pragmatic tendency to dissolve all abstractions into effects, making it possible to put forth seriously arguments that political force could balance or counter or circumscribe industrial power, apparently somewhat in the manner of one vector mathematically canceling another. By reducing everything to social activity of one sort or another, dissimilar attributes were made commensurable. Assertions about the state or, for that matter, private agencies creating freedom thereby acquired superficial plausibility. In short, the prior and primordial inclination to find the essence of reality in the stream of social processes manifested itself in the identification of liberty with selected values and preferred results, most preeminently socioeconomic equality, the disaffirmation of the purely political origin of such terms as taxation and monopoly, among others, and the habitual and confusing interchange of a myriad of governmental and societal concepts. The state, its coercive features swept aside, was now seen as contending with voluntary associations for the execution of the same social functions.

CONCLUSION

Although it is always a hazardous enterprise to judge the degree of influence exerted by an idealogy, it would not be an exaggeration to allege that the concept of "free society" gradually managed to drive out that of "free government." Admittedly, progressives often did not obtain in practice what they had sought in theory. Still, the fundamental preconceptions that lay at the base of empirical collectivism slowly permeated the various sectors of the community, becoming the self-evident catchwords of the scholar's treatise, church sermon, newspaper editorial, and political proclamation. One potent measure of the intellectual success of progressives is that even their opponents, in many instances, accepted the basic premises formulated by them, if not the exact conclusions which they drew from these premises. Another is that American political thought over the last sixty years has largely, if at times unconsciously, moved within the ideational confines of empirical collectivism, whose essentials had been fully set forth by the time the United States entered the First World War. Indeed, succeeding writers in the tradition have added little, if anything, new to it. Certain ideas have been greatly elaborated; interest groups, for instance, have been made the subject of an entire literature. On the whole, nevertheless, no concepts have been developed that depart radically from the synthesis achieved in this period.

It must be emphasized that the ideological victory which crowned the efforts of reformers was not achieved through an explicit, frontal assault on republicanism. On the contrary, most advocates of democratic collectivism, in the course of their attack on the essence of free government, were quick to avow that they were loyal to the spirit, if not the letter, of republican doctrine. They continued to use the very terms, such as equality, democracy, freedom, the public interest, monopoly, and rights, that the republicans had employed in their analysis. Superficial plausibility could thereby be attached to the assertion that the "new" individualism was merely a rational adaptation of the "old" individualism to different conditions. The use of the same terminology, however, concealed the fact that an entirely novel content had been given to the concepts in question. Dissolved in a sea of turbulent social activity, they now signified desirable results or processes. This replacement of political by social categories, which has been traced here, constituted the essential meaning of progressive individualism and led quite naturally to constant entreaties that government be freed from the artificial chains preventing it from acting in the interests of society.

Not all the criticisms made by progressives were without foundation. There was justice, for instance, in their accusations that government had often become the tool of wealth and that the Supreme Court was exceeding its authority in interpreting the "due process" clause of the Fourteenth Amendment in a substantive, not merely a procedural, sense. Nor is it to be averred that any expansion of the power of the state was necessarily inconsonant with republicanism. Many of the measures supported by progressives were not without merit, and perhaps reformers were correct, to a certain degree, when they chided some of their opponents for sticking unimaginatively to the status quo. The important point, however, is that reformers justified even their more meritorious proposals in language hostile to the philosophy of free government, arguing, among other things, that they would result in a more equal distribution of property or reflect the will of social forces, or satisfy the requirements of the "new rights." Workman's compensation laws or legislation regulating working conditions could have been sanctioned through a further development of the concept of a property right. But progressives instead explicitly introduced the standard of an illimitable, all-inclusive "social interest" (or "good of the whole") superseding "abstract" individual rights.[1] The boundary line between the private and the public need not have remained static: yet they made no attempts to show that the proposals in question were either strictly constitutional or compatible with personal or property rights.

The progressive doctrines, whatever their intrinsic merits, were not always set forth with clarity and consistency. The prevailing attitude that a process of formal definition simply could not capture an elusive "social reality" no doubt had some effect on the manner in which reformers presented their ideas. In any case, rigor was eschewed in favor of a rather diffusive approach to the issues. Indeed, "loose ends" abounded. Many ideas were greatly in need of both elaboration and clarification. Thus, although the argument that the state could avoid force and that voluntary transactions among individuals could be coercive rested on the assumption that concepts could be reduced to effects, no extended analysis was made of the mechanics of the immaterial "force." It also is paradoxical that, on the one hand, selected social relationships were denounced as exploitative and, on the other, that "society," presumably embodying such relationships among others, could be safely called upon to use the state, as well as other organizations, in exercising its will. Again, altruism was adduced as one justification for redistributing wealth through taxation; yet, logically altruism presupposes a prior ascertainment of what the true good for man consists in, and this ascertainment reformers failed to provide. They merely assumed what they needed to prove. All told, although progressives produced an abundance of ideas, they did not always engage in a systematic and complete analysis of them. Omissions, seeming paradoxes, and vagueness were part of the legacy they bequeathed to their successors.

One tendency of democratic collectivism that has been largely ignored in this discussion should be briefly mentioned here—the "elitism" that seemed to characterize the attitudes of many, if not all, proponents of free society. Even if the equation of wealth to power (or desirable attributes) were to be accepted, it is clear that few critics of constitutional government were maintaining that all men be equalized in "power." Inequalities were to be reduced, though not completely eliminated. In so far as they were not done away with and because no standard existed by which to determine precisely and objectively which distribution of wealth was to prevail, the way was clear for some men to act as the guardians of society, both shaping desires and deciding which ones were to be satisfied at the expense of others. Democracy, of course, was not rejected. Nevertheless, it was often assumed that the inchoate yearnings of the masses needed to be directed into the proper channels. Although such elitism was seldom made explicit, it can be manifestly found in many writings of the period. It is particularly evident, for example, in Lester Ward's sociocracy and Herbert Croly's Progressive Nationalism.

The intellectual revolution wrought by advocates of free society had a lasting and detrimental impact on American political thought. If it is still too early to say whether irreparable damage has been done, it is quite clear that only a telling and exhaustive critique of progressivism has any chance at all of resurrecting free government. In short, a philosophical counterattack entailing an incisive analysis of the progressive premises, definitions, assumptions, methodology, and conclusions is absolutely necessary. Such an intellectual offensive must demonstrate that society is an aggregate, not a whole or an ineffable mystery, perfectly understandable in terms of the individuals who comprise it; the public interest consequently refers only to predefined and limited state functions. It would prove that the stock phrase "elastic constitution" is nothing more than an oxymoron, that laws become tyrannical when nonspecific, and that alleged precedents are not to be construed as justifications for expanding the polity beyond its proper boundaries. Refuting the fallacy that capital is either fixed or a communal product or both, it must emphasize that because individuals create wealth and economic opportunities, one man does not profit at the expense of another where force and fraud are outlawed; the riches of the truly productive are not the cause of anyone's poverty and ultimately expand the opportunities and raise the productivity of the other segments of society. It must delineate the close parallels between the fantasies of "true religion," on the one hand, and "just" prices, "reasonable" rates of profit, and "perfect" competition, on the other. It should further reveal that rights appertain to the freedom to pursue, that an individual's right to property is not in the least violated if his efforts to acquire property in the desired degree are not successful, and that property rights, as possessions of human beings, not only do not conflict with human rights but are properly to be classed among them. Dismissing the belief that freedom is to be equated with range of choice, prosperity, equality, or any particular value matrix, whether that of an individual or collective, it would fix its meaning in physical terms. It would cast aside a moral code which sacrifices ability to need and implacably condemn a politics premised on interest groups demanding their "fair share" of the "national" wealth.

It would show not only that much of the reasoning used to legitimize arbitrary inroads upon property can be extended to vindicate encroachments upon "personal" freedom as well but that even without formal prescriptions laid upon freedom of expression, government control of property may, in endlessly subtle and not so subtle ways, seriously affect the distribution of ideas and direct opinion into preconceived molds. Most importantly, denying the key maxims of the pragmatist epistemology, it would render spurious that sine qua non of progressive argumentation and perorations, namely, the incoherent jumbling together of political and social abstractions; entities are not dissolvable into processes and behavior; concepts are not to be identified promiscuously with effects, and especially effects taken out of context; and the purported dichotomy of the practical and theoretical is simply nonexistent. Throughout this comprehensive appraisal, inconsistencies, shifting use of language, ambiguities, non sequiturs, and arbitrary suppositions would be exposed. The end result would see free government reclaiming as its own those terms expropriated in the progressive revolution and rescuing theory from the sterile and unprofitable track onto which it had been shunted after the Civil War. But most of all, the path would then be opened for Americans to regain an opportunity once lost and to make, in the words of the Massachusetts Bill of Rights, that "recurrence to fundamental principles" which was so characteristic of the old liberalism at its best, renewing in the process the valuable elements in their heritage.

NOTES
SELECTED BIBLIOGRAPHY
INDEX

NOTES

Introduction

1. Arthur Ekirch, *The Decline of American Liberalism* (New York, 1955), chaps. 8, 9.

2. Henry Commager, *The American Mind* (London, 1950), pp. 338, 341; Sidney Fine, *Laissez Faire and the General Welfare State* (Ann Arbor, Mich., 1956), pp. 12-14, 24, 30, 376, 382. This view is also taken by Edward R. Lewis, *A History of American Political Thought from the Civil War to the First World War* (New York, 1937), p. 364.

3. Charles Merriam, *American Political Ideas* (New York, 1923), pp. 3, 338; Ralph Gabriel, *The Course of American Democratic Thought* (New York, 1940), pp. 159, 214, 332, 334; Merle Curti, *The Growth of American Thought* (New York, 1943), pp. 611-12, 629.

4. Louis Hartz, *The Liberal Tradition in America* (New York, 1955), pp. 148, 177, 197, 219, 229-30, 233-34. For a similar interpretation, see Yehoshua Arieli, *Individualism and Nationalism in American Thought* (Cambridge, Mass., 1946), pp. 121, 178, 194, 197, 322.

5. Vernon L. Parrington, *Main Currents in American Thought* (New York, 1930), p. xiv; Daniel Aaron, *Men of Good Hope* (New York, 1951), pp. 18, 251, 308; Robert McCloskey, *American Conservatism in the Age of Enterprise* (Cambridge, Mass., 1951), pp. 2-7, 15; Ekirch, *Decline of Liberalism*, pp. 194, 197. It is to be noted that McCloskey nowhere offers a coherent definition of conservatism, other than to claim that the doctrines of Sumner and other opponents of economic democracy were "organically related to earlier thinking that had been conventionally regarded as conservative" (p. x). The closest he comes to a positive definition is when he states that conservatives defended the property right above all else (p. 22).

6. The actual term "individualism" appears not be have been used by republican theorists, although John Taylor frequently alluded to "individuality." As Friedrich Hayek observes, both the terms "individualism" and "socialism" seem to have been introduced by the Saint-Simonians (Hayek, *Individualism and Economic Order* [Chicago, 1972], p. 3).

7. On Locke as seen through the eyes of eighteenth-century English writers and men of affairs preoccupied with "corruption" and "influence," consult Bernard Bailyn, *The Origin of American Politics* (New York, 1958), pp. 39-57.

8. See, for example, Charles McIlwain, *Constitutionalism and the Changing World* (Cambridge, Eng., 1939), pp. 244-45. At this point, I should also note that the distinction I make between liberalism and democracy is that I use the former in a general way to refer to limitations on political power based on the notion of individual rights, whereas the latter is made to signify only the participation of the people in government. Republican individualism was

both democratic and liberal, yet no necessary connection exists between the two concepts. Thus, one may be a liberal without being a democrat, and vice versa. Cf. Friedrich Hayek, *The Constitution of Liberty* (Chicago, 1960), pp. 104-5. As for the much used and abused term "conservatism," in so far as I employ it in its adjectival form, I shall be referring only to an attitude which is suspicious of rapid change and values stability. Conservatism as an ideology, however, sets up resistance to change and stability as ideals per se and tends to justify the existing state of affairs.

9. Collectivism may be distinguished from socialism. The latter, in so far as it is not qualified by such adjectives as "broad," "general," "unorthodox," etc., or by the context in which it is employed, will be used to mean state ownership of the tools of production, distribution, and exchange. Collectivism is a more generic term. I will use it to refer to the doctrine that assumes the real existence of a supraindividual organism or structure, advocates that society control all the affairs of the nation for the benefit of the "people as a whole," and regards the concentration of extensive powers in the state over persons and property as the primary means by which society would exercise its rule.

10. Pragmatism has been variously defined and, indeed, Arthur Lovejoy has distinguished at least thirteen different views that have been featured under the label of "pragmatic" (*The Thirteen Pragmatisms and Other Essays* [Baltimore, 1963]). Charles Peirce felt it imperative to differentiate his thought from that of William James and adopted the term "pragmaticism" to characterize his philosophy. For the purposes of this study, however, I shall not find it necessary to distinguish sharply among the varieties of pragmatism, although I shall note how Dewey was able to combine ideas from Peirce and James. Basically, by "pragmatic," I will mean an outlook which perceives change as the very essence of reality. From this fundamental attitude can be deduced several corollaries. First, theoretical considerations are eschewed as failing to embody a changing reality and allegedly practical standards are substituted for them. Experience detached from reality becomes the fount of knowledge. Second, a historical relativism is affirmed, and absolutes in philosophy and politics are rejected. Plurality replaces the "block universe." Finally, as suits a philosophy of change, the meaning of concepts is found in the effects or consequences which logically issue from them. Process emerges superior to fixity.

CHAPTER I

1. Thomas Paine, *The Rights of Man* (1791; rpt. Garden City, N.Y., 1961), p. 305.

2. Arieli, *Individualism in American Thought*, p. 85.

3. McCloskey, *American Conservatism*, p. 15.

4. Jefferson as quoted in Adrienne Koch, *The Philosophy of Thomas Jefferson* (New York, 1943), p. 175; Joseph Dorfman, "The Economic Philosophy of Thomas Jefferson," *Political Science Quarterly* 55 (1940):105.

5. Koch, *Philosophy of Jefferson*, p. 182. Some ambiguity is attached to

Jefferson's position, however. He did not write any formal political treatise, and his political views are gleaned for the most part from his correspondence. He did make a distinction between natural and civil rights and considered property as one of the latter. But if property rights are regarded as a corollary of natural rights, as the "application of the general principle that man had a natural right" to use his faculties (see Arieli, *Individualism in American Thought*, p. 131), then it is difficult to see wherein the conflict between the two lay. Jefferson was never clear as to the exact nature of the distinction and its practical ramifications, and it does not occupy any important place in his thought, especially as compared to his numerous private and public utterances affirming the sanctity of private property and the dangers of an energetic government. Furthermore, what prompted Jefferson to make this distinction originally was his analysis of feudal society in France, where the acquisition and transmission of property was governed, not by free contract, but by the varied political restrictions of the ancien régime. Jefferson protested that in this case the laws of property violated natural right, and his successful efforts to abolish feudal restrictions in his native state are well known. On this whole issue, see Adrienne Koch, *Jefferson and Madison* (New York, 1950), pp. 78-81.

6. Thomas Paine, *The Complete Writings of Thomas Paine*, ed. Philip S. Foner, 2 vols. (New York, 1945), 2:558; Paine, *Rights of Man*, p. 434; James Madision, *Letters and Other Writings of James Madison*, 4 vols. (Philadelphia, 1865), 4: 478. See also Madison's comment: "Conscience is the most sacred of all property" (*The Complete Madison*, ed. Saul K. Padover [New York, 1953], p. 268).

7. John Taylor, *Construction Construed and Constitutions Vindicated* (Richmond, 1820), pp. 12-13, 73-74, 204, 208, 239, 265-66. See, as well, his observation that "I discern no difference between pension, and alien and sedition laws, in principle. All depend upon the doctrine, that congress have a mysterious power, to act upon persons and things, beyond the definitions of the constitution" (p. 253).

8. Madison, *Complete Madison*, p. 37.

9. Cf. John Taylor, *An Inquiry into the Principles and Policy of the Government of the United States* (Fredericksburg, Va., 1814), p. 113: "I consider those possessions as property which are fairly gained by talents and industry, or are capable of subsisting, without taking property from others by law."

10. H. B. Parkes, *The American Experience* (New York, 1955), p. 161.

11. John Taylor, for instance, maintained that John Adams's system, as he interpreted it, reduced orders to two: the recipients of benefits extorted by the state and the victims who had their property confiscated by the state. Violent animosities, he also claimed, would arise between rich and poor, once the pernicious principle is introduced that the government can allocate property by law (*Inquiry*, pp. 113-15, 563). Paine similarly concluded that the "riots and tumults" in England were not caused by the absence of government, but its presence, for it was the "generating cause" of these disturbances (*Rights of Man*, p. 401).

12. Taylor, *Inquiry*, p. 397; Taylor, *Construction Construed*, pp. 208, 234, 267. See also his comment that the "scope and design of this treatise, is to maintain the right of every body to get money, and I only differ with the capitalists, by

proceeding to assert, that every one has a further right to use it for his own benefit, because he has earned it" (*Construction Construed*, p. 238).

13. Thomas Jefferson, *The Life and Selected Writings of Thomas Jefferson*, ed. Adrienne Koch and William Peden (New York, 1944), pp. 319, 330, 437; Koch, *Jefferson and Madison*, p. 111; Madison, *Complete Madison*, pp. 268-69; Madison, *Writings*, 3:648. For a general discussion of Madison's viewpoint on these matters, see Edward M. Burns, *James Madison* (New Brunswick, N.J., 1938), pp. 47-59.

14. Paine, *Complete Writings*, 2:405, 409, 559; Paine, *Rights of Man*, pp. 458-59, 476, 480, 493-94. See also Eric Foner, *Tom Paine and Revolutionary America* (New York, 1976), chap. 5.

15. See Arieli, *Individualism in American Thought*, pp. 159-60. Consult also Burns, *James Madison*, p. 48, who contends that Madison adopted laissez-faire principles with "numerous modifications."

16. Paine, *Rights of Man*, p. 482; Taylor, *Inquiry*, p. 617; Jefferson, *Selected Writings*, pp. 262-63; Madison, *Complete Madison*, pp. 313-14; Koch, *Jefferson and Madison*, pp. 257, 262.

17. As one example, consult Paine, *Complete Writings*, 2:413. See also Burns, *James Madison*, p. 50, and Madison, *Complete Madison*, p. 198. Both Jefferson and Madison went beyond the views of those like John Taylor who believed that internal improvements fell properly only within the domain of the states by insisting that the national government ought to undertake such projects.

18. This argument was repeated again and again by advocates of republicanism. See, for instance, Jefferson's comment that the minds of the people must be improved to make republican government safe (*Selected Writings*, p. 265) and Madison's observation that a "well-instructed people alone can be permanently a free people" (Koch, *Jefferson and Madison*, p. 257).

19. Madison, *Writings*, 3:648-53.

20. Jefferson as quoted in Koch, *Jefferson and Madison*, pp. 65-66; Paine, *Complete Writings*, 1:611-13, 617.

21. Such a scheme, then, is fundamentally different from those which would give individuals "access" to artificial means of production, that is, those produced by human effort, such as factories. The contrast is between a limited, natural resource whose existence was not brought about by the endeavors of individual men and products that were brought into being only through the application of human labor.

22. Madison, *Complete Madison*, p. 273. See, in addition, Madison's revealing reply to Littleton Dennis Teackle regarding his possible membership in an organization favorable to governmental regulation of trade on an extended scale (*Writings*, 3:441).

23. For instance, Paine commented that equality "consists in the enjoyment of the same rights by each" and that the law should be the same for all (*Complete Writings*, 2:559). Taylor conceived of equality as one of "moral rights and duties" (Henry H. Simms, *Life of John Taylor* [Richmond, 1932], p. 136).

24. See Madison, *Complete Madison*, p. 46; Jefferson, *Selected Writings*, p. 266.

25. Madison, *Complete Madison*, p. 45. Note also Jefferson's explicit rejection of an "elective despotism" (*Selected Writings*, p. 237).

26. Jefferson had proposed, for example, that the validity of legal enact-

ments might be limited to the generation that wrote them. In this way, the living would not be beholden to the dead. But Madison perspicaciously pointed out that republican theory required the consent of every individual to majority rule and that if such consent could not be given implicitly, either every law would have to be renewed when a new member entered the body politic or his express consent would have to be obtained. The only tenable solution, Madison argued, was that a "*tacit* assent may be given to established Governments and laws, and that this assent is to be inferred from the omission of an express revocation" (*Complete Madison*, p. 32).

27. Paine, *Complete Writings*, 2:372.

28. Jefferson as quoted in Koch, *Jefferson and Madison*, p. 64.

29. Quoted in Eugene T. Mudge, *The Social Philosophy of John Taylor of Caroline* (New York, 1939), p. 162. See also Madison's comment that the "profit of each is the wealth of the whole" (*Complete Madison*, p. 272).

30. Taylor as quoted in Mudge, *Philosophy of Taylor*, p. 161.

31. On this, Taylor as cited in Simms, *Life of Taylor*, p. 155.

32. Madison, *Complete Madison*, p. 33.

33. Edward S. Corwin, *The 'Higher Law' Background of American Constitutional Law* (Ithaca, N.Y., 1955), p. 89. Also, consult Paine, *Rights of Man*, p. 309.

34. Taylor, *Construction Construed*, p. 164. Note also his comment that "constitutions are only previous supreme laws, which antecedently repeal all subsequent laws, contrary to their tenor" (p. 135).

35. Paine, *Complete Writings*, 2:523.

36. Isabel Patterson, *The God of the Machine* (Caldwell, Idaho, 1968), p. 162.

37. Taylor, *Construction Construed*, p. 165; Taylor as quoted in Mudge, *Philosophy of Taylor*, p. 168; on Jefferson, see Koch, *Jefferson and Madison*, p. 111; Madison, as cited in Koch, *Jefferson and Madison*, p. 128; Madison, *Complete Madison*, p. 197; Burns, *James Madison*, pp. 111-13.

38. Taylor, *Construction Construed*, p. 284; Madison as quoted in Claude Bowers, *Jefferson and Hamilton* (London, 1925), p. 76.

39. Paine, *Rights of Man*, p. 432

40. See Ekirch, *Decline of Liberalism*, pp. 79-82.

41. Taylor, *Construction Construed*, pp. 77-78.

42. The viewpoints of Jefferson and Madison were so closely allied that what is called Jeffersonianism (in the narrow sense) is, in fact, greatly indebted to Madison for many of its most important theoretical formulations. See Koch, *Jefferson and Madison*, p. vii, and Burns, *James Madison*, pp. 89-90. Still, such major figures as John Taylor and Thomas Paine held opinions which were at variance with certain key elements of the Madisonian outlook. The former adhered to a strict states' rights position (with all the consequences ensuing therefrom) and a more rigid version of laissez-faire, portraying the protective tariff as both unconstitutional and an attack on property. The latter rejected the elaborate and ingenious mechanisms posited by Madison for the preservation of free government, reduced governmental branches to the legislative and the executive, did not distinguish sharply between a republic and a democracy, and optimistically maintained that a constitution in itself was a sufficient check on any despotic tendencies which might arise. See Mudge, *Philosophy of Taylor*, pp. 106-41;

Simms, *Life of Taylor*, p. 182; Taylor, *Construction Construed*, pp. 71, 135, 159; with respect to Paine, consult Foner, *Paine and America*, pp. 90-91; Paine, *Complete Writings*, 2: 524, 526-28, 586, 588; Paine, *Rights of Man*, p. 387.

43. Hartz, *Liberal Tradition*, chap. 2.

44. John Adams, *Works*, ed. Charles F. Adams, 10 vols. (Boston, 1850-56), 6:7-9, 65. Adams, after having "composed [his] risible muscles," wrote a series of letters to John Taylor, justifiably denying Taylor's accusation that he had intended to equalize property among orders (Simms, *Life of Taylor*, pp. 140, 144).

45. Leonard White, *The Federalists* (New York, 1948), chap. 8.

46. George Fitzhugh, *Sociology for the South* (Richmond, 1854), p. 26; John C. Calhoun, *A Disquisition on Government and Selections from the Discourse*, ed. C. Gordon Post (New York, 1953), p. 45.

47. Alan P. Grimes, *American Political Thought* (New York, 1960), pp. 202-10.

48. Henry D. Thoreau, *Walden and On the Duty of Civil Disobedience* (rpt. New York, 1960), p. 223; Emerson as quoted in Henry D. Gray, *Emerson* (Stanford, Calif., 1917), p. 82.

49. Ralph Waldo Emerson, *Essays* (New York, 1926), pp. 409, 415, 419; Thoreau, *Duty of Civil Disobedience*, pp. 222-23, 236, 240.

50. Madison, *Complete Madison*, p. 314.

51. Madison recognized this, noting that he did not know of a "better service that could be rendered to the science of political economy than a judicious explanation of the cases constituting exceptions to the principle of free industry, which, as a general principle, has been so unanswerably established" (ibid., p. 274).

CHAPTER II

1. William Graham Sumner, *What Social Classes Owe to Each Other* (New York, 1883), p. 98; John W. Burgess, *The Reconciliation of Government with Liberty* (New York, 1915), pp. 368-69, 371-72; Field as quoted in Carl B. Swisher, *Stephen J. Field, Craftman of the Law* (Washington, D.C., 1930), p. 379

2. See John Fiske, *Civil Government in the United States* (Boston, 1904), p. 3; Edwin L. Godkin, *Problems of Modern Democracy* (New York, 1896), pp. 228-30; Fine, *General Welfare State*, p. 58. Even Sumner, the most uncompromising liberal of this period, cited laissez-faire only as a general maxim and supported public education, the subsidization of paupers and the physically incapacitated, and factory legislation (*Essays of Willaim Graham Sumner*, ed. Albert G. Keller and Maurice R. Davies, 2 vols. [New Haven, 1934], 1:476, 482; 2:475-77; Sumner, *Social Classes*, p. 20; Sumner, *Folkways* [Boston, 1913], p. 628).

3. William Graham Sumner, *Earth-Hunger and Other Essays*, ed. Albert G. Keller (New Haven, 1913), p. 122; Godkin, *Problems of Democracy*, p. 229.

4. Holmes as quoted in Lawrence Evans and Charles Fenwick, *Cases on American Constitutional Law* (Chicago, 1938), p. 1084; Richard T. Ely, *The Past and the Present of Political Economy (Baltimore, 1884), p. 26.*

5. For instance, although Fiske identified the common interest with the

sphere of the state, considering the government as the "directing or managing of such affairs as concern all the people," he did not provide a definition of those objects which were of interest to all citizens (*Civil Government*, p. 3).

6. Godkin as quoted in Alan Grimes, *The Political Liberalism of the New York Nation, 1865-1932* (Chapel Hill, N.C., 1953), p. 24; John W. Burgess, "The Ideal of the American Commonwealth," *Political Science and Comparative Constitutional Law*, 2 vols. (Boston, 1890-91), 1:176.

7. For example, Harris E. Starr points out that the "rather widespread opinion that Sumner was a disciple of Herbert Spencer is more than half-false. He neither owed as much to Spencer nor was in as close agreement with him as is generally assumed" (Starr, *William Graham Sumner* [New York, 1925], pp. 392-96).

8. Consult Grimes, *American Political Thought*, p. 293, who states that Godkin and his collaborators combined utilitarianism and natural rights theory.

9. See Swisher, *Field*, esp. chap. 16.

10. John W. Burgess, *Reminiscences of an American Scholar* (New York, 1934), p. 253.

11. Ibid., p. 252; Burgess, *Political Science and Law*, 1:88, 175, 177.

12. Burgess, *Political Science and Law*, 1:52-53, 57, 175; John W. Burgess, "Private Corporations from the Point of View of Political Science," *Political Science Quarterly* 13 (1898):210.

13. Burgess, *Political Science and Law*, 1:57.

14. Ibid., p. 176; Burgess, "Private Corporations," p. 211.

15. Edwin L. Godkin, *Reflections and Comments, 1865-1895* (New York, 1895), p. 233.

16. Godkin, *Problems of Democracy*, pp. 228-29.

17. Ibid., pp. 161-62; Godkin, *Reflections and Comments*, pp. 232-33.

18. Godkin, *Problems of Democracy*, pp. 172-73.

19. Richard Hofstadter, *Social Darwinism in American Thought* (New York, 1955), pp. 51-53.

20. Sumner, *Essays*, 2:95.

21. See Edward L. Youmans, ed., *Herbert Spencer on the Americans and the Americans on Herbert Spencer* (New York, 1883), no pagination.

22. For Sumner's antimetaphysical attitude, consult Starr, *Sumner*, pp. 525-26.

23. As quoted in Fine, *General Welfare State*, p. 131, n. 16.

24. Sumner, *Earth-Hunger*, pp. 165, 198; Sumner, *Social Classes*, p. 34; Sumner, *Essays*, 1:473.

25. Sumner, *Essays*, 1:170. See also his comment: "There are no dogmatic propositions which are universally and always true: there are views which prevail, at a time, for a while, and then fade away and give place to other views" (1:86).

26. Ibid., 2:103; see also Sumner, *Social Classes*, p. 135.

27. Sumner, *Essays*, 1:364.

28. Sumner, *Social Classes*, p. 163.

29. For instance, Gabriel, *Course of American Thought*, p. 233; Stow Persons, *American Minds* (New York, 1958), p. 245.

30. Sumner, *Social Classes*, pp. 33, 124; Sumner, *Essays*, 1:87, 481, 2:143-49.

31. Sumner, *Social Classes*, pp. 39, 113, 118, 121-22, 157, 165, 168-69. See as well his frank letter to workingmen in the *New Haven Register*, Oct. 14, 1880 (Starr, *Sumner*, p. 242).

32. Sumner, *Essays*, 1:24-25, 2:435.

33. Ibid., 2:260; Sumner, *Social Classes*, p. 156.

34. Sumner, *Social Classes*, p. 119; Sumner, *Essays*, 1:17, 93, 101, 178; 2:18; Sumner, *Folkways*, p. 201; Sumner, *Earth-Hunger*, p. 203. Sumner comments in *Folkways* that ideals "often interfere in the second state of the sequence-act, thought, act . . . In fact, the real process in great bodies of men is not one of deduction from any great principle of philosophy or ethics. It is one of minute efforts to live well under existing conditions" (p. 38).

35. Sumner, *Folkways*, p. 4; see also Sumner, *Essays*, 1:362.

36. Sumner, *Folkways*, p. 29.

37. Sumner, *Essays*, 1:105-6.

38. Burgess, *Reconciliation*, p. 380.

39. Elihu Root, *Addresses on Government and Citizenship* (Cambridge, Mass., 1916), pp. 70-72, 539; William H. Taft, *Present Day Problems* (New York, 1908), pp. 178, 219; Franklin H. Giddings, *Democracy and Empire* (New York, 1901), p. 153.

40. See, for example, Root, *Addresses*, pp. 79, 540.

41. Ibid., p. 540.

42. Arthur T. Hadley, *Economics* (New York, 1896), p. 15.

43. Root, *Addresses*, pp. 85-86; Giddings, chapter on "Industrial Democracy"; Taft, *Present Day Problems*, pp. 124-33. Those who totally opposed free government could argue, of course, that there was no reason why the state should not speed the process along.

44. Herbert Spencer, *The Man versus the State*, ed. Truxton Beale (New York, 1916).

CHAPTER III

1. Ekirch, *Decline of Liberalism*, p. 170.

2. For a discussion of this whole issue in the European context, see Friedrich Hayek, *The Counter-Revolution of Science* (New York, 1955), esp. pp. 36-63. By metaphysical, or ontological, collectivism, I shall mean the assumption that a collective, such as society, constitutes a physical whole. Epistemological collectivism will be understood to mean the belief that knowledge is obtained through the functioning of a collective mind, the consciousness of the reified collective.

3. Charles Peirce, *Chance, Love, and Logic*, ed. Morris Cohen (New York, 1923), pp. 56-58.

4. See Edward C. Moore, *American Pragmatism: Peirce, James, and Dewey* (New York, 1961), pp. 70-72.

5. Elisha Mulford, *The Nation* (Boston, 1889), pp. 9, 11; Orestes A. Brownson, *The American Republic*, in *Works*, collected and arranged by Henry F. Brownson, 20 vols (New York, 1882-87; rpt. 1966), 18:15, 38-39.

6. Henry Jones Ford, *The Natural History of the State* (Princeton, N.J., 1915), pp. 173-74; James W. Garner, *Introduction to Political Science* (New York, 1910), p. 65; Harry Elmer Barnes, *Sociology and Political Theory* (New York, 1924), p. 27.

7. Thus, Woodrow Wilson referred to both government and society as living structures (*The New Freedom* [New York, 1913], pp. 47-48).

8. Woodrow Wilson, *The State* (Boston, 1889), p. 597; John Bates Clark, *The Philosophy of Wealth* (Boston, 1886), p. 38; Henry C. Adams, *The Relation of the State to Industrial Action*, Publications of the American Economic Association, vol. 1, no. 6 (1887) pp. 30-31; Walter Weyl, *The New Democracy* (New York, 1912), p. 162; Henry D. Lloyd, *Wealth against Commonwealth* (New York, 1894), p. 497; Herbert Croly, *Progressive Democracy* (New York, 1915), pp. 195-97.

9. Eric Goldman, *Rendezvous with Destiny* (New York, 1963), pp. 97-98; Joseph Dorfman, *The Economic Mind in American Civilization*, 5 vols. (New York, 1946-59), 3:148-49.

10. Dorfman, *Economic Mind*, 3:147.

11. Murray Rothbard, *Man, Economy, and State* (Los Angeles, 1970), p. 933, n. 68.

12. Lester Ward, *Pure Sociology* (New York, 1911), p. 555; Lester Ward, *The Psychic Factors of Civilization* (Boston, 1893), p. 323; Lester Ward, *Outlines of Sociology* (New York, 1899), p. 186. Ward also commented: "It [society] should imagine itself as an individual, with all the interests of an individual, and becoming fully *conscious* of these interests it should pursue them with the same indomitable will with which the individual pursues his interests. Not only this, it must be guided, as he is guided, by the social *intellect*" (*Psychic Factors*, p. 324).

13. Ward, *Psychic Factors*, p. 276.

14. Thus, as we have seen, Herbert Croly spoke of "centres of association" which could be "fitted" into society.

15. Arthur F. Bentley, *The Process of Government* (Chicago, 1908), pp. 220-22.

16. Bentley seemed to equate activity with social relationships among men (ibid., p. 176).

17. Ibid., p. 177.

18. Barnes, *Sociology and Political Theory*, pp. 6, 9, 107; Garner, *Introduction to Political Science*, p. 292; Albion W. Small, "Fifty Years of Sociology in the United States, 1865-1915," *American Journal of Sociology* 21 (1916):723.

19. Lester Ward, *Dynamic Sociology*, 2 vols. (New York, 1897), 1:519, 578.

20. Henry George, *Progress and Poverty* (New York, 1883), especially books 6-9. Edward Bellamy was one of those who expressed his wonderment that those reformers who talked about the "unearned increment" in land did not widen their criticism so as to embrace the entirety of economic action (Bellamy, *Equality* [New York, 1897], chap. 13).

21. Bellamy, *Equality*, chap. 11, 12; Edward Bellamy, *Looking Backward*, ed. John L. Thomas (Cambridge, Mass. 1967), chap. 1.

22. Herbert Croly, *The Promise of American Life* (New York, 1909), p. 380; Lloyd, *Wealth against Commonwealth*, pp. 494, 512.

23. James Allen Smith, *The Spirit of American Government* (New York, 1907), p. 402; Thorstein Veblen, *The Theory of Business Enterprise* (New York, 1904), p. 291; Weyl, *New Democracy*, p. 83.

CHAPTER IV

1. See Lewis, *History of American Thought*, p. 515; Merriam, *American Political Ideas*, pp. 426-27; Gabriel, *Course of American Thought*, p. 364; Goldman, *Rendezvous with Destiny*, pp. 159-60; Commager, *American Mind*, pp. 326-28; Ekirch, *Decline of Liberalism*, p. 182.

2. Smith as quoted in Goldman, *Rendezvous with Destiny*, p. 159.

3. On "reform Darwinism," see Goldman, *Rendezvous with Destiny*.

4. See Philip Wiener, *Evolution and the Founders of Pragmatism* (Cambridge, Mass., 1949), esp. pp. 191-97. Cf. John Dewey, *The Influence of Darwin on Philosophy* (New York, 1910), pp. 1-19, 77-111, 198-239.

5. See Burleigh T. Wilkins, "James, Dewey, and Hegelian Idealism," *Journal of the History of Ideas* 17 (1956):332-46; Gabriel, *Course of American Thought*, p. 336; Commager, *American Mind*, p. 99; Wiener, *Founders of Pragmatism*, p. 103.

6. Hofstadter, *Social Darwinism*, p. 135.

7. William James, *Pragmatism* (New York, 1907), p. 201; William James, *The Meaning of Truth* (New York, 1909), p. 165.

8. See Moore, *American Pragmatism*, p. 163.

9. Moore observes that Dewey "does not think we start from a knower, a knowing, and a known" (ibid., p. 190).

10. James, *Pragmatism*, pp. 197-203, 248-59; John Dewey, *Essays in Experimental Logic* (Chicago, 1916).

11. Washington Gladden, *The New Idolatry* (New York, 1905), p. 201.

12. Brownson, *Works*, 18:15-18; Mulford, *Nation*, pp. 74-75, 106.

13. Barnes, *Sociology and Political Theory*, pp. 6, 146; Roscoe Pound, "The End of Law as Developed in Juristic Thought," *Harvard Law Review* 27 (1914):624; Ward, *Dynamic Sociology*, 1:31-32; Westel W. Willoughby, *The Nature of the State* (New York, 1896), p. 181; Westel W. Willoughby, *Social Justice* (New York, 1900), pp. 22, 226; Ford, *History of State*, pp. 176-77; Oliver W. Holmes, Jr., *Collected Legal Papers* (New York, 1921), p. 173.

14. Weyl, *New Democracy*, p. 161.

15. Ward, *Dynamic Sociology*, 1:519; Bellamy, *Equality*, chap. 17; John Dewey and James Tufts, *Ethics* (New York, 1908), p. 445. All references to the last work are drawn from the sections written exclusively by Dewey.

16. Dewey and Tufts, *Ethics*, p. 441.

17. Weyl, *New Democracy*, pp. 161-62; Walter Lippmann, *Drift and Mastery* (New York, 1914), p. 109.

18. Pound, "End of Law in Juristic Thought," pp. 619, 626-27.

19. Roscoe Pound, "The End of Law as Developed in Legal Rules and Doctrines," *Harvard Law Review* 27 (1914):225-26; Roscoe Pound, "Interests of Personality," *Harvard Law Review* 28 (1915):343-44, 347, 349; Roscoe Pound, "Legislation as a Social Function," *American Journal of Sociology* 18 (1913):760.

20. Roscoe Pound, "Justice according to Law," *Columbia Law Review* 14 (1914):119.

21. Wilson, *New Freedom*, p. 274; Theodore Roosevelt, *The Works of Theodore Roosevelt*, ed. Hermann Hagedorn, 20 vols. (New York, 1925), 19:28.

22. Roscoe Pound, "The Scope and Purpose of Sociological Jurisprudence," *Harvard Law Review* 25 (1911):143.

23. Mulford, *Nation*, p. 149.

24. Oliver W. Homes, Jr., *The Common Law* (Boston, 1881), p. 1.

25. Lester Ward, *Applied Sociology* (New York, 1906), pp. 16, 27; Willoughby, *Nature of State*, p. 340; Dewey and Tufts, *Ethics*, p. 476; Roosevelt, *Works*, 17:307.

26. Wilson, *New Freedom*, pp. 6-7, 10, 15, 22, 57.

27. Henry Demarest Lloyd, *Lords of Industry* (New York, 1910), p. 145; Lloyd, *Wealth against Commonwealth*, pp. 494-95.

28. Frank J. Goodnow, *Politics and Administration* (New York, 1900), p. 2; Frank J. Goodnow, *Social Reform and the Constitution* (New York, 1911), pp. 5-6, 11-13; Frank J. Goodnow, "The Constitutionality of Old Age Pensions," *American Political Science Review* 5 (1911):205.

29. Bellamy, *Looking Backward*, chap. 5.

30. Thorstein Veblen, *The Instinct of Workmanship* (New York, 1922), pp. 234-35, 237n; Veblen, *Theory of Enterprise*, pp. 79, 274-75, 283, 376.

31. Lippmann, *Drift and Mastery*, p. 164; Charles R. Van Hise, *Concentration and Control* (New York, 1912), p. 257.

32. Charles Beard, *An Economic Interpretation of the Constitution of the United States* (New York, 1913), p. 18; Smith, *Spirit of Government*, pp. 291-93, 298-99.

33. Smith, *Spirit of Government*, pp. 304-8.

34. Weyl, *New Democracy*, pp. 108-9, 43, 45, 162.

35. Croly, *Promise of Life*, pp. 44-45, 49, 153, 183.

CHAPTER V

1. Lewis, *History of American Thought*, p. 364. Cf. Gabriel, *Course of American Thought*, p. 225.

2. Roscoe Pound, "Liberty of Contract," *Yale Law Journal* 18 (1909):484.

3. Richard T. Ely, *Socialism* (New York, 1894), p. 351; Aaron, *Men of Good Hope*, p. 162.

4. Ward as quoted in Commager, *American Mind*, p. 208.

5. Dewey and Tufts, *Ethics*, pp. 472, 481.

6. Wilson, *State*, p. 661.

7. Weyl, *New Democracy*, p. 288; Brooks Adams, *The Theory of Social Revolutions* (New York, 1913), p. 17; Lippmann, *Drift and Mastery*, pp. 54, 62, 82.

8. Bellamy, *Looking Backward*, chap. 5; Bellamy, *Equality*, chap. 3; Lloyd, *Wealth against Commonwealth*, pp. 1, 312, 511-12, 514.

9. Goodnow, *Politics and Administration*, p. 18; Weyl, *New Democracy*, pp. 108-20; Wilson, *New Freedom*, p. 48.

10. Ward, *Psychic Factors*, p. 304; Croly, *Progressive Democracy*, pp. 212, 231;

Evans and Fenwick, *Cases on Law*, p. 1084; Wilson, *New Freedom*, p. 48; Smith, *Spirit of Government*, pp. 27-124, 305.

11. Wilson, *New Freedom*, p. 4.

12. Weyl, *New Democracy*, p. 194. See also Dewey's definition that "if democracy has a moral and ideal meaning, it is that a social return be demanded from all and that opportunity for development of distinctive capacities be afforded all" (Dewey, *Democracy and Education* [New York, 1916], p. 142).

13. The limited intervention that many republicans supported, of course, was not justified by reference to democratic norms.

14. Bellamy, *Looking Backward*, chap. 5; Weyl, *New Democracy*, p. 163.

15. Ekirch, *Decline of Liberalism*, p. 194.

16. Lewis, *History of American Thought*, pp. 349, 351.

17. Henry George, *Social Problems* (New York, 1883), pp. 176-78, 188; see also Fine, *General Welfare State*, pp. 293-94; Aaron, *Men of Good Hope*, pp. 86-90.

18. Bellamy, *Looking Backward*, chaps. 5, 22; Bellamy, *Equality*, chap. 2.

19. Ward, *Psychic Factors*, pp. 264-65; Lloyd, *Wealth against Commonwealth*, passim; Lloyd, *Lords of Industry*, p. 194 and passim.

20. Adams, *Relation of State*, pp. 34-35, 38, 44.

21. William Jennings Bryan, *Speeches of William Jennings Bryan*, 2 vols. (New York, 1909), 2:139-40; Louis Brandeis, *Other People's Money* (New York, 1914), p. 160; Wilson, *New Freedom*, pp. 172-73, 180; Weyl, *New Democracy*, pp. 281-82.

22. Richard T. Ely, *Monopolies and Trusts* (New York, 1900), p. 213; Richard T. Ely, *Property and Contract*, 2 vols. (New York, 1914), 1:359; Ely, *Socialism*, pp. 262, 272; John Bates Clark, *The Distribution of Wealth* (New York, 1902), p. 3; John Bates Clark and John Maurice Clark, *The Control of Trusts* (New York, 1912), pp. 200-210; Roosevelt, *Works*, 17:310, 19:15, 18; Van Hise, *Concentration and Control*, chap. 5; Weyl, *New Democracy*, pp. 84, 94, 283; Croly, *Promise of Life*, pp. 359, 369; Lippmann, *Drift and Mastery*, p. 84.

23. For a competent treatment of the inability of legislators and the courts to arrive at a reasonably specific definition of "restraint of trade," see A. D. Neale, *The Antitrust Laws of the United States of America* (Cambridge, Eng., 1960), esp. pp. 11-30.

24. Patterson, *God of Machine*, pp. 182-83.

CHAPTER VI

1. Roosevelt, *Works*, 19:24: Edward A. Ross, *Sin and Society* (New York 1907), pp. 147-48; Willoughby, *Nature of State*, p. 340; Ely, *Property and Contract*, 1:165, 172, 176, 207, 224; Ward, *Psychic Factors*, pp. 202-3; Waite as cited in Evans and Fenwick, *Cases on Law*, p. 1135; Barnes, *Sociology and Political Theory*, p. 6; Weyl, *New Democracy*, pp. 281n, 295.

2. Ely, *Socialism*, p. 3; Vernon P. Bodein, *The Social Gospel of Walter Rauschenbusch and Its Relation to Religious Education* (New Haven, 1944), pp. 64-67.

3. See, for example, William E. Walling, *Progressivism—And After* (New York, 1914).

4. Raymond G. Gettell, *History of American Political Thought* (New York, 1928), p. 584; Grimes, *American Political Thought*, pp. 362, 386; Richard Hofstadter, *The American Political Tradition* (New York, 1951), p. 49; Fine, *General Welfare State*, p. 329; Merriam, *American Political Ideas*, p. 461. Notice also should be taken of Roscoe Pound's remark that "in compelling study of the relation of law to social classes and so making for a socialization of the law, the group of socialist jurists has done a considerable service" ("Scope and Purpose of Jurisprudence," *Harvard Law Review* 25[1912]:502).

5. Thus, Richard Ely observed that genuine reform aimed at the improvement of all classes; (*Socialism*, p. 7); and Veblen's "socialism" exalted the community, not the workers (Aaron, *Men of Good Hope*, p. 237).

6. As one example, consult Weyl, *New Democracy*, chap. 12.

7. See, for instance, Clark, *Philosophy of Wealth*, p. 199. For arguments of a similar nature advanced by economist John R. Commons, consult Dorfman, *Economic Mind*, 3:280.

8. Ward, *Psychic Factors*, p. 330; Croly, *Progressive Democracy*, p. 217; Weyl, *New Democracy*, chap. 12.

9. Bentley, *Process of Government*, pp. 165-68.

10. James, *Pragmatism*, p. 200; Dewey, *Essays in Logic*, p. 330; Peirce as quoted in Moore, *American Pragmatism*, p.55. On Peirce, see also Wiener, *Founders of Pragmatism*, p. 92.

11. Wilson, *New Freedom*, p. 48; Lloyd, *Wealth against Commonwealth*, pp. 3-4; Lippmann, *Drift and Mastery*, pp. 294-95.

12. Veblen, *Theory of Enterprise*, p. 319; Ward, *Dynamic Sociology*, 1:61; Holmes as quoted in Evans and Fenwick, *Cases on Law*, p. 1084; Pound, "Scope and Purpose of Jurisprudence," *Harvard Law Review* 25 (1912):516; Pound, "Liberty of Contract," p. 462; Goodnow, *Reform and Constitution*, p. 3.

13. Such was the view, for instance, of Walter Rauschenbusch (Bodein, *Social Gospel of Rauschenbusch*, p. 99).

14. Weyl, *New Democracy*, p. 279.

15. Irving Fisher, "Why Has the Doctrine of Laissez Faire Been Abandoned?" *Science*, 4 Jan. 1907, p. 18; Lippmann, *Drift and Mastery*, pp. 108-9; Pound, "Scope and Purpose of Jurisprudence," *Harvard Law Review* 25 (1912):146. On the Brandeis brief, see Goldman, *Rendezvous with Destiny*, p. 139.

16. On the interrelationship of facts and concepts, cf. Talcott Parsons, *The Structure of Social Action*, 2 vols. (New York, 1968), 1:28.

17. For a critique of the identification of the meaning of concepts with consequences, see Bland Blanshard, *Reason and Analysis* (LaSalle, Ill., 1973), pp. 192-97.

18. Croly, *Promise of Life*, pp. 387, 390; Croly, *Progressive Democracy*, pp. 380-81; Weyl, *New Democracy*, p. 292.

19. See, for instance, Ross, *Sin and Society*, esp. pp. 140-51.

20. Bellamy, *Looking Backward*, chaps. 5, 15, 19; Bellamy, *Equality*, chap. 24.

21. Ward, *Dynamic Sociology*, 1:12, 35; Ward, *Outlines of Sociology*, p. 166.

22. Ward, *Outlines of Sociology*, p. 274; Ward, *Dynamic Sociology*, 1:37; Ward, *Psychic Factors*, pp. 306, 326-27.

23. Pound, "End of Law in Rules and Doctrines," pp. 226, 228.

24. Weyl, *New Domocracy*, chap. 13, pp. 163, 276; Lippmann, *Drift and Mastery*, esp. pp. 71, 168.

25. Bentley, *Process of Government*, pp. 165, 206, 208-9, 212.

26. Even the younger generation of economists rebelled against what they considered to be abstract formulas, insisting on an inductive and pragmatic approach. Consult Fine, *General Welfare State*, p. 204; Commager, *American Mind*, p. 235.

27. Willoughby, *Nature of State*, p. 330.

28. As one example, consult Willoughby, *Social Justice*, p. 229.

29. Evans and Fenwick, *Cases on Law*, p. 1134; Wilson, *State*, pp. 638-40.

30. Goodnow, "Constitutionality of Pensions," pp. 194, 210-11.

31. Wilson, *State*, p. 651; Edmund J. James, *The Relation of the Modern Municipality to the Gas Supply*, Publications of the American Economic Association, vol. 1, nos. 2, 3 (1886), p. 38; Charles H. Cooley, *Social Organization* (New York, 1912), p. 403; Garner, *Introduction to Political Science*, p. 321; Willoughby, *Nature of State*, pp. 314, 338-39; Ward, *Dynamic Sociology*, 1:61.

CHAPTER VII

1. Smith, *Spirit of Government*, p. 305.

2. Roscoe Pound, "Mechanical Jurisprudence," *Columbia Law Review* 8 (1908):616.

3. Roosevelt as quoted in Goldman, *Rendezvous with Destiny*, p. 189; Croly, *Promise of Life*, p. 409.

4. Weyl, *New Democracy*, p. 292.

5. Ward, *Pure Sociology*, p. 568; Ward, *Psychic Factors*, p. 275; Lloyd, *Wealth against Commonwealth*, p. 527; Wilson, *New Freedom*, pp. 281, 284.

6. Ford, *History of State*, p. 177.

7. Ward, *Dynamic Sociology*, 1:63.

8. This was a position explicitly adopted by Henry C. Adams (see Dorfman, *Economic Mind*, 3:374).

9. Lloyd, *Wealth against Commonwealth*, p. 3; Lloyd, *Lords of Industry*, pp. 183-84, 197, 207-8.

10. Adams, *Relation of State*, p. 48; James, *Relation of Municipality*, p. 8; Wilson, *New Freedom*, p. 222.

11. For a dissection of some of the common fallacies involved in the application of the term "monopoly" to private corporations, see Rothbard, *Man and State*, pp. 560-660; Ludwig von Mises, *Human Action* (Chicago, 1966), pp. 277-87, 360-77.

12. Ely, *Socialism*, p. 282; William J. Ghent, *Our Benevolent Feudalism* (New York, 1902), p. 9; Ward, *Dynamic Sociology*, 1:39; Croly, *Promise of Life*, pp. 187, 202.

13. Bentley, *Process of Government*, pp. 268, 296-97.

14. Ward, *Psychic Factors*, pp. 323-24; Adams, *Theory of Revolutions*, pp. 17, 21; Clark and Clark, *Control of Trusts*, pp. 12-13.

15. Charles W. Eliot, *The Conflict between Individualism and Collectivism in a Democracy* (New York, 1910), p. 16; Lippmann, *Drift and Mastery*, pp. 50-51.

16. Lloyd, *Wealth and Commonwealth*, p. 12; James, *Relation of Municipality*, p. 35.

17. Pound, "Liberty of Contract," p. 463; Veblen, *Instinct of Workmanship*, p. 296; Veblen, *Theory of Enterprise*, p. 277; Weyl, *New Democracy*, pp. 164, 323n.

18. Bellamy as cited in Aaron, *Men of Good Hope*, p. 111.

19. Dewey, *Democracy and Education*, p. 347.

20. Weyl, *New Democracy*, p. 160.

21. Fine, *General Welfare State*, p. 170; Hofstadter, *Social Darwinism*, p. 108.

22. Lyman Abbott, *Christianity and Social Problems* (Boston, 1897), p. 81; Washington Gladden, *Applied Christianity* (Cambridge, Mass., 1886), pp. 33, 35; Walter Rauschenbusch, *Christianity and the Social Crisis* (New York, 1910); Walter Rauschenbusch, *Christianizing the Social Order* (New York, 1912).

23. See, for instance, George D. Herron, *Between Caesar and Jesus* (New York, 1899), for the view that the Christ's teachings were essentially communistic.

24. William D. P. Bliss, ed., *The Encyclopaedia of Social Reforms* (New York, 1897), p. 1266; Lloyd, *Wealth against Commonwealth*, p. 504; on Bellamy, see Aaron, *Men of Good Hope*, p. 123.

25. Willoughby, *Social Justice*, pp. 31, 251; Willoughby, *Nature of State*, p. 350; William Dean Howells, *A Traveler from Altruria* (New York, 1895); Wilson, *State*, p. 659; Bellamy, *Equality*, chap. 3; Bellamy as cited in Arthur E. Morgan, *Edward Bellamy* (New York, 1944), p. viii; Croly, *Promise of Life*, pp. 49, 418; Lloyd, *Wealth against Commonwealth*, pp. 494, 514; Ward, *Dynamic Sociology*, 1:14; Ward, *Pure Sociology*, p. 571. Ward, it might be added, was usually imprecise in his definition of society, but in his *Applied Sociology* (p. 326), he was more ingenuous: "They [the masses] only want power—the power that is theirs of right and which lies within their grasp. They have only to reach out and take it. The victims of privative ethics are in the immense majority. They constitute society."

26. Out of 116 economists and sociologists who replied to a questionnaire shortly after the turn of the century, 59 had studied in Germany between 1873 and 1905 (Jurgen Herbst, *The German Historical School in American Scholarship* [Ithaca, 1965], p. 130).

27. Irving Fisher stated that this was one of the erroneous postulates of the classical theory which led the new economists to invoke state action ("Why Has Laissez Faire Been Abandoned," pp. 18-27). Cf. Willoughby, *Nature of State*, p. 327.

28. Richard T. Ely, *Social Aspects of Christianity and Other Essays* (New York, 1889), p. 6; Ely, *Past and Present*, p. 64; Clark, *Philosophy of Wealth*, pp. 37-38, 44-45, 56.

29. Dewey and Tufts, *Ethics*, pp. 387-88, 482-83. For similar equivocations, see Ward, *Dynamic Sociology*, 1:522-23; Ward, *Outlines of Sociology*, pp. 104-8.

30. Croly, *Promise of Life*, p. 186.

31. Ward, *Dynamic Sociology*, 2:233; Croly, *Promise of Life*, p. 206; on Ross, Bernhard J. Stern, ed., "The Ward-Ross Correspondence, 1891-1896," *American Sociological Review* 3 (1938):364; Ely, *Socialism*, pp. 207-8. Cf. Wilson, *New Freedom*, pp. 282-83.

32. Bliss, *Encyclopaedia of Reforms*, p. 1274.

33. Ward, *Dynamic Sociology*, 1:32.

34. Dewey and Tufts, *Ethics*, p. 438.

35. Ward, *Applied Sociology*, p. 23; Dewey and Tufts, *Ethics*, p. 484.

36. Bellamy, *Equality*, chaps. 11, 12; Bellamy, *Looking Backward*, chaps. 6, 17.

37. Dewey and Tufts, *Ethics*, pp. 483-84.

38. Abbott, *Christianity and Social Problems*, pp. 57-58; Gladden, *Applied Christianity*, pp. 14, 37; Lippmann, *Drift and Mastery*, p. 115; Simon N. Patten, *The New Basis of Civilization* (New York, 1907), p. 9; Croly, *Progressive Democracy*, p. 382; Croly, *Promise of Life*, pp. 23, 370; Weyl, *New Democracy*, pp. 163, 294-95. See also Lloyd, *Wealth against Commonwealth*, p. 524.

CONCLUSION

1. Thus, Roscoe Pound wrote that the basis of workman's compensation legislation was the "social interest in the full moral and social life of the individual in classes that are less able to bear the burdens of injuries incident to their task" ("End of Law in Rules and Doctrines," p. 233); and Walter Weyl suggested that the reduction of the hours of the working day could be legitimized if it were to the *"net ultimate advantage of the whole community"* (*New Democracy*, p. 150).

SELECTED BIBLIOGRAPHY

Aaron, Daniel. *Men of Good Hope*. New York: Oxford University Press, 1951.

Abbott, Lyman. *Christianity and Social Problems*. Boston: Riverside Press, 1897.

——. *The Spirit of Democracy*. Boston: Houghton Mifflin Co., 1910.

Adams, Brooks. *The Theory of Social Revolutions*. New York: Macmillan Co., 1913.

Adams, Henry. *The Degradation of the Democratic Dogma*. New York: Macmillan Co., 1919.

Adams, Henry C. *The Relation of the State to Industrial Action*. Publications of the American Economic Association, vol. 1, no. 6. 1887.

Anderson, Thornton. *Brooks Adams*. Ithaca: Cornell University Press, 1951.

Arieli, Yehoshua. *Individualism and Nationalism in American Thought*. Cambridge: Harvard University Press, 1964.

Barnes, Harry Elmer. *Sociology and Political Theory*. New York: Alfred Knopf, 1924.

——. "Two Representative Contributions of Sociology to Political Theory: The Doctrines of William Graham Sumner and Lester Frank Ward." *American Journal of Sociology* 25 (1919): 1-23, 150-70.

Beard, Charles A. *An Economic Interpretation of the Constitution of the United States*. New York: Macmillan Co., 1913.

——. *The Myth of Rugged American Individualism*. New York: John Day Co., 1931.

Bellamy, Edward. *Equality*. New York: D. Appleton and Co., 1897.

——. *Looking Backward*. Ed. John L. Thomas. Cambridge: Harvard University Press, 1967.

Bentley, Arthur F. *The Process of Government*. Chicago: University of Chicago Press, 1908.

——, and Dewey, John. *John Dewey and Arthur Bentley: A Philosophical Correspondence, 1932-1951*. Ed. Jules Altman and Sidney Ratner. New Brunswick: Rutgers University Press, 1964.

Brandeis, Louis. *Other People's Money*. New York: Frederick Stokes Co., 1914.

Brownson, Orestes A. *Works*. 20 vols. Collected and arranged by Henry F. Brownson. 1882-87; rpt. New York: AMS Press, 1966.

Bryan, William J. *Speeches of William Jennings Bryan*. 2 vols. New York: Funk and Wagnalls Co., 1909.

Burgess, John W. *Political Science and Comparative Constitutional Law*. 2 vols. Boston: Ginn and Co., 1890-91.

——. *The Reconciliation of Government with Liberty*. New York: Charles Scribner's Sons, 1915.

——. *Reminiscences of an American Scholar*. New York: Columbia University Press, 1934.

Burns, Edward M. *James Madison*. New Brunswick: Rutgers University Press, 1938.

Chamberlain, John. *Farewell to Reform*. New York: Liverwright, 1932.

Clark, John B. *The Distribution of Wealth*. New York: Macmillan Co., 1902.

——. *The Philosophy of Wealth*. Boston: Ginn and Co., 1886.

——, and Clark, John M. *The Control of Trusts*. New York: Macmillan Co., 1912.

Commager, Henry. *The American Mind*. London: Oxford University Press, 1950.

Cook, Thomas, and Leavelle, A. B. "German Idealism and American Theories of the Democratic Community." *Journal of Politics* 5 (1943):213-36.

Cooley, Charles H. *Human Nature and the Social Order*. New York: Charles Scribner's Sons, 1902.

——. *Social Organization*. New York: Charles Scribner's Sons, 1912.

Croly, Herbert. *Progressive Democracy*. New York: Macmillan Co., 1915.

——. *The Promise of American Life*. New York: Macmillan Co., 1909.

Curti, Merle. *The Growth of American Thought*. New York: Harper and Brothers, 1943.

Destler, Chester M. *American Radicalism, 1865-1901*. New York: Octagon Books, 1965.

Dewey, John. *Democracy and Education*. New York: Macmillan Co., 1916.

——. *The Early Works, 1882-1898*. 5 vols. London: Southern Illinois University Press, 1967.

——. *The Influence of Darwin on Philosophy*. New York: Henry Holt and Co., 1910.

——, and Tufts, James. *Ethics*. New York: Henry Holt and Co., 1908.

Dorfman, Joseph. *The Economic Mind in American Civilization*. 5 vols. New York: Viking Press, 1946-59.

——. *Thorstein Veblen and His America*. New York: Viking Press, 1934.

Egbert, Donald D., and Persons, Stow, eds. *Socialism and American Life*. 2 vols. Princeton: Princeton University Press, 1952.

Ekirch, Arthur. *The Decline of American Liberalism*. New York: Longmans, Green, and Co., 1955.

Elliott, William Y. *The Pragmatic Revolt in Politics*. New York: Macmillan Co., 1928.

Ely, Richard T. *Ground under Our Feet*. New York: Macmillan Co., 1938.

——. *Monopolies and Trusts*. New York: Macmillan Co., 1900.

——. *The Past and the Present of Political Economy*. Baltimore: N. Murray, 1884.

——. *Property and Contract*. 2 vols. New York: Macmillan Co., 1914.

——. *Social Aspects of Christianity, and Other Essays*. New York: Thomas Y. Crowell and Co., 1894.

——. *Socialism*. New York: Thomas Y. Crowell and Co., 1894.

Faulkner, Harold U. *The Decline of Laissez Faire, 1897-1917*. New York: Rinehart, 1951.

Fine, Sidney. *Laissez Faire and the General Welfare State*. Ann Arbor: University of Michigan Press, 1956.

Fiske, John. *American Political Ideas*. New York: Harper and Brothers, 1885.

——. *Civil Government in the United States*. Boston: Houghton, Mifflin, And Co., 1904.

Foner, Eric. *Tom Paine and Revolutionary America*. New York: Oxford University Press, 1976.

Ford, Henry Jones. *The Natural History of the State*. Princeton: Princeton University Press, 1915.

Freund, Ernst. *The Police Power*. Chicago: Callaghan and Co., 1904.

Gabriel, Ralph. *The Course of American Democratic Thought*. New York: Ronald Press Co., 1956.

Garner, James W. *Introduction to Political Science*. New York: American Book Co., 1910.

George, Henry. *Progress and Poverty*. New York: D. Appleton and Co., 1883.

——. *Social Problems*. New York: National Single Tax League, 1883.

Ghent, William J. *Our Benevolent Feudalism*. New York: Macmillan Co., 1902.

Giddings, Franklin H. *Democracy and Empire*. New York: Macmillan Co., 1901.

——. *The Principles of Sociology*. New York: Macmillan Co., 1896.

Gladden, Washington. *Applied Christianity*. Cambridge: Riverside Press, 1886.

——. *Social Facts and Forces*. New York: G. P. Putnam's Sons, 1897.

Godkin, Edwin L. *Problems of Modern Democracy*. New York: Charles Scribner's Sons, 1896.

——. *Reflections and Comments, 1865-1895*. New York: Charles Scribner's Sons, 1895.

——. *Unforseen Tendencies of Democracy.* New York: Houghton, Mifflin, and Co., 1898.

Goldman, Eric, *Rendzevous with Destiny.* New York: Alfred Knopf, 1963.

Goodnow, Frank J. *Politics and Administration.* New York: Macmillan Co., 1900.

——. *Social Reform and the Constitution.* New York: Macmillan Co., 1911.

Grimes, Alan P. *American Political Thought.* New York: Holt, Rinehart, and Winston, 1960.

——. "The Pragmatic Course of Liberalism." *Western Political Quarterly* 9 (1956):633-40.

Gronlund, Lawrence. *The Cooperative Commonwealth.* Boston: Lee and Shepard, 1884.

Hadley, Arthur T. *Economics.* New York: G. P. Putnam's Sons, 1896.

Hartz, Louis. *The Liberal Tradition in America.* New York: Harcourt, Brace, and Co., 1955.

Henderson, Charles. *Social Duties.* Chicago: University of Chicago Press. 1909.

——. *The Social Spirit in America.* New York: Flood and Vincent, 1897.

Herbst, Jurgen. *The German Historical School in American Scholarship.* Ithaca: Cornell University Press, 1965.

Hicks, John D. *The Populist Revolt.* Minneapolis: University of Minnesota Press, 1931.

Hofstadter, Richard. *Social Darwinism in American Thought.* New York: George Braziller, 1955.

Holmes, Oliver W., Jr. *Collected Legal Papers.* New York: Harcourt, Brace, and Co., 1921.

Hook, Sidney. *John Dewey, an Intellectual Portrait.* New York: John Day Co., 1939.

Hopkins, Charles H. *The Rise of the Social Gospel in American Protestantism, 1865-1915.* New Haven: Yale University Press, 1940.

James, Edmund. *The Relation of the Modern Municipality to the Gas Supply.* Publications of the American Economic Association, vol. 1, nos. 2, 3. 1886.

James, William. *The Meaning of Truth.* New York: Longmans, Green, and Co., 1898.

——. *Pragmatism.* New York: Longmans, Green, and Co., 1907.

Jefferson, Thomas. *The Life and Selected Writings of Thomas Jefferson.* Ed. Adrienne Koch and William Peden. New York: Modern Library, 1944.

Keller, Albert G. *Reminiscences (Mainly Personal) of William Graham Sumner.* New Haven: Yale University Press, 1933.

Koch, Adrienne. *The Philosophy of Thomas Jefferson*. New York: Columbia University Press, 1943.

La Follette, Robert M. *Autobiography*. Madison: University of Wisconsin Press, 1960.

Lewis, Edward R. *A History of American Political Thought from the Civil War to the World War*. New York: Macmillan Co., 1937.

Lippmann, Walter, *Drift and Mastery*. New York: Mitchell Kennerley, 1914.

———. *A Preface to Politics*. New York: Mitchell Kennerley, 1913.

Loewenberg, Bert J. "Darwinism Comes to America, 1859-1900." *Mississippi Valley Historical Review* 28 (1941):339-68.

Lloyd, Henry D. *Lords of Industry*. New York: G. P. Putnam's Sons, 1910.

———. *Wealth against Commonwealth*. New York: Harper and Brothers, 1894.

Madison, Charles A. *Critics and Crusaders*. New York: Henry Holt and Co., 1947.

Madison, James. *The Complete Madison*. Ed. Saul K. Padover. New York: Harper and Brothers, 1953.

———. *Letters and Other Writings of James Madison*. 4 vols. Philadelphia: J. P. Lippincott and Co., 1865.

Mason, Alpheus T. "American Individualism: Fact and Fiction." *American Political Science Review* 46 (1952):1-18.

Mathur, G. B. "Hume and Kant in Their Relation to the Pragmatic Movement." *Journal of the History of Ideas* 16 (1955):198-208.

McCloskey, Robert G. *American Conservatism*. Cambridge: Harvard University Press, 1951.

Merriam, Charles E. *American Political Ideas*. New York: Macmillan Co., 1923.

Miller, Perry. *American Thought, Civil War to World War I*. New York: Rinehart and Co., 1957.

Moore, Edward C. *American Pragmatism: Peirce, James, and Dewey*. New York: Columbia University Press, 1961.

Mowry, George E. *Theodore Roosevelt and the Progressive Movement*. Madision: University of Wisconsin Press, 1946.

Mulford, Elisha. *The Nation*. Boston: Houghton, Mifflin, and Co., 1889.

Oberholtzer, Ellis P. *A History of the United States since the Civil War*. 5 vols. New York: Macmillan Co., 1926-37.

Paine, Thomas. *The Complete Writings of Thomas Paine*. Ed. Philip S. Foner. 2 vols. New York: Citadel Press, 1945.

Parkes, H. B. *The American Experience*. New York: Alfred Knopf, 1955.

Parrington, Vernon L. *Main Currents in American Thought*. New York: Harcourt, Brace, and Co., 1930.

Patten, Simon N. *The New Basis of Civilization.* New York: Macmillan Co., 1907.

——. *The Theory of Social Forces.* Supplement, vol. 7. Philadelphia: American Academy of Political and Social Science, 1896.

Patterson, Isabel. *The God of the Machine.* Caldwell, Idaho: Caxton Printing, 1968.

Peirce, Charles S. *Chance, Love, and Logic.* Ed. Morris Cohen. Harcourt, Brace, and Co., 1923.

——. *Collected Papers of Charles Sanders Peirce.* 8 vols. Cambridge: Harvard University Press, 1931-58.

Perry, Ralph Barton. *The Thought and Character of William James.* 2 vols. Boston: Little, Brown, and Co., 1935.

Persons, Stow. *American Minds.* New York: Henry Holt, 1958.

Pound, Roscoe. "The End of Law as Developed in Juristic Thought." *Harvard Law Reveiw* 27 (1914):605-28.

——. "Interests of Personality." *Harvard Law Review* 28 (1915):343-65.

——. "The Scope and Purpose of Sociological Jurisprudence." *Harvard Law Review* 24-25 (1911-12): 591-619, 140-68, 489-516.

Roosevelt, Theodore. *The Works of Theodore Roosevelt.* 20 vols. Ed. Hermann Hagedorn. New York: Charles Scribner's Sons, 1925.

Root, Elihu. *Addresses on Government and Citizenship.* Cambridge: Harvard University Press, 1916.

Ross, Edward A. *Foundations of Sociology.* New York: Macmillan Co., 1905.

——. *Seventy Years of It.* New York: D. Appleton-Century Co., 1936.

——. *Sin and Society.* New York: Houghton, Mifflin Co., 1907.

Seligman, Edwin R. A. *The Economic Interpretation of History.* New York: Columbia University Press,1917.

Shields, Currin. "The American Tradition of Empirical Collectivism." *American Political Science Review* 46 (1952):104-20.

Simms, Henry H. *Life of John Taylor.* Richmond: William Byrd Press, 1932.

Small, Albion. *Between Eras: From Capitalism to Democracy.* Chicago: Victor Bruder, 1913.

——. "Fifty Years of Sociology in the United States (1865-1915)." *American Journal of Sociology* 21 (1916):721-864.

Smith, James Allen. *The Spirit of American Government.* New York: Macmillan Co., 1907.

Spencer, Herbert. *The Man versus the State.* Ed. Truxton Beale. New York: Mitchell Kennerley, 1916.

Starr, Harris E. *William Graham Sumner.* New York: Henry Holt, 1925.

Sumner, William Graham. *Earth-Hunger and Other Essays.* Ed. Albert G. Keller. New Haven: Yale University Press, 1913.

———. *Essays of William Graham Sumner.* 2 vols. Ed. Albert G. Keller and Maurice R. Davie. New Haven: Yale University Press, 1934.

———. *Folkways.* Boston: Ginn and Co., 1913.

———. *The Forgotten Man and Other Essays.* Ed. Albert G. Keller. New Haven: Yale University Press, 1918.

———. *What Social Classes Owe to Each Other.* New York: Harper and Brothers, 1883.

Swisher, Carl B. *Stephen J. Field, Craftsman of the Law.* Washington, D.C.: Brookings Institution, 1930.

Taft, William H. *Present Day Problems.* New York: Dodd, Mead, and Co., 1908.

Taylor, John. *Construction Construed and Constitutions Vindicated.* Richmond: Shepard and Pollard, 1820.

———. *An Inquiry into the Principles and Policy of the Government of the United States.* Fredericksburg: Green and Cady, 1814.

———. *New Views of the Constitution of the United States.* Washington, D.C.: Way and Gideon, 1823.

Townshend, Harvey. *Philosophical Ideas in the United States.* New York: American Books Co., 1934.

Van Hise, Charles R. *Concentration and Control.* New York: Macmillan Co., 1912.

Veblen, Thorstein. *Instinct of Workmanship.* New York: B. W. Huebsch, 1914.

———. *The Theory of Business Enterprise.* New York: Charles Scribner's Sons, 1904.

———. *The Theory of the Leisure Class.* Boston: Houghton, Mifflin Co., 1913.

Walling, William E. *Progressivism—and After.* New York: Macmillan Co., 1914.

Ward, Lester. *Applied Sociology.* New York: Ginn and Co., 1906.

———. *Dynamic Sociology.* 2 vols. New York: D. Appleton and Co., 1897.

———. *Glimpses of the Cosmos.* 6 vols. New York: G. P. Putnam's Sons, 1913-18.

———. *Outlines of Sociology.* New York: Macmillan Co., 1899.

———. *Psychic Factors of Civilization.* Boston: Ginn and Co., 1893.

———. *Pure Sociology.* New York: Macmillan Co., 1911.

Weyl, Walter. *The New Democracy.* New York: Macmillan Co., 1912.

White, Leonard. *The Federalists.* New York: Macmillan Co., 1948.

White, Morton, *Pragmatism and the American Mind.* New York: Oxford University Press, 1973.

Wiener, Philip. *Evolution and the Founders of Pragmatism.* Cambridge: Harvard University Press, 1949.

Wilkins, Burleigh T. "James, Dewey, and Hegelian Idealism." *Journal of the History of Ideas* 17 (1956):332-46.

Willoughby, Westel. *The Nature of the State*. New York: Macmillan Co., 1896.

——. *Social Justice*. New York: Macmillan Co., 1900.

Wilson, Woodrow. *Constitutional Government in the United States*. New York: Columbia University Press, 1908.

——. *The New Freedom*. New York: Doubleday, Page, and Co., 1913.

——. *The State*. Boston: D. C. Heath and Co., 1889.

Woolsey, Theodore D. *Political Science*. 2 vols. New York: Charles Scribner's Sons, 1877.

Youmans, Edward L., ed. *Herbert Spencer on the Americans and the Americans on Herbert Spencer*. New York: D. Appleton and Co., 1883.

INDEX